"SELL YOUR GARMENT AND BUY A SWORD"

DID JESUS PERMIT RETALIATION AGAINST RELIGIOUS VIOLENCE?

SECOND EDITION

"Sell Your Garment and Buy a Sword"

Did Jesus permit retaliation against religious violence?

Second Edition

Mipo E. Dadang, Ph. D.

AFRICA CHRISTIAN TEXTBOOKS

2017

"Sell Your Garment and Buy a Sword"
Did Jesus permit retaliation against religious violence?
Second Edition
© 2017 Mipo E. Dadang

Africa Christian Textbooks (ACTS)

ACTS Bookshop, International HQ, TCNN,
PMB 2020, Bukuru, Plateau State, 930008, Nigeria
GSM: +234 (0) 803-589-5328; E-mail: pa@actsnigeria.org
Website: http://actsnigeria.org

ISBN: 9789789053674 Print
ISBN: 9789789053681 ePub
ISBN: 9789789053698 Mobi

DEDICATION

This book is dedicated to: Pius A. Akubo (Senior Advocate of Nigeria), Mrs. Esther Pius, Barrister Joseph B. Danboyi, Mrs. Florence Joseph, Mr. Gyet Yem, Mrs. Hadiza Gyet, Dr. Peter S. Abdu, Mrs. Helen Peter, Rev, Stephen B. Panya, Mrs. Naomi Stephen. Mrs. Deborah Dadang, and Miss Keziah Zhumnan Mipo Dadang

Cast your cares on the Lord
and He will sustain you;
He will never let the righteous fall.

—Psalm 55:22

CONTENTS

Foreword v

Abbreviations 1

Preface vii

1. Religion and Violence 3

2. Overview of Nigeria 15

3. Mission Work in West Africa 21

4. Understanding Religious Violence 31

5. Human Violence in Scripture 41

6. Religion and Peace Building 59

7. Early Church Response 65

8. Biblical Response to Religious Violence 73

Bibliography 83

FOREWORD

Throughout history the Christian Church (or body of Christ) and individual Christians have often faced violent persecution. From its emergence in the Book of Acts, the Body of Christ continues to exist only because God has said that the gates of hell shall not prevail against it. Nevertheless, violence against Christians remains the reality of their existence. Many Christians find it difficult to understand why they are subjected to violent attack in Nigeria and other parts of the world. How should the Christians properly respond to the violence meted out against them? Over the centuries, responses have ranged from pacifist to violent retaliation, often in defense of what was previously their domain.

The situation in Northern Nigeria has been remarkable with violent attacks on Christians being a frequent occurrence since the late 1980s. Christian responses at the beginning were largely pacifist, expecting State authorities to deal with the situation. However, the State failed to defend the Christians and the subsequent Christian response has been to resort to counter-violence in self-defense. From the turn of the twentieth century to the present, violent confrontations between Muslims and Christians in Northern Nigeria have been part of our unfortunate experience. Some of these responses to violence have been explained by those involved as owing to the fact that there are no longer any "cheeks" left to turn Some "Christians" have used the excuse that there are no longer any "cheeks" left to turn to explain their violent responses to violence! We are now confronted with the reality that the identity of being followers of Jesus Christ, the Prince of Peace, is in danger of being lost and with it, the Christian witness to the world of the truth that is in Jesus Christ. There is an urgent need, therefore, to understand and explain what the Christian response should be biblically.

This is the task that the author has undertaken in this very important book. In this important study, he has called attention to the urgent need for Christians to return to the Bible and find the answer as to how to respond to violence and, more importantly, continue with the task of witnessing to the unsaved - the primary purpose they are on earth for. It is clear to me that we need more voices than solely Dr. Dadang's on this matter to call the Church from being distracted and even destroyed from within by uninformed people engaging in our "Christian" response to violence. Fortunately, this well researched work goes a long way in helping Christians in Northern Nigeria, and beyond, to find their way back to the Bible on this issue. If they should remain followers of Christ, Christians must first understand what the Lord Jesus says in the Bible, about what our response should be bearing in mind the main assignment Christ has given us. Dr. Dadang has done a splendid job in assisting with the materials from which the body of Christ is able to reflect deeply on this issue and to carefully listen to what the Lord is commanding. As we come to that understanding, we would do well to obey God so that we can continue to be the salt and light to the world.

Therefore, I have the honor as an ordinary Christian to urge all like me, and the Pastors and Theologians among us to engage in family discussions, teaching, and exposition of the truth of the Bible on this issue. This way we will recover the ground lost to the devil and shine the light of Christ as we should.

Professor Istifanus Sonsare Zabadi

PREFACE

Everyone needs to know that the Creator is the author of life. Any person or thing that God creates should not be thoughtlessly destroyed. We should always seek to save, preserve, and restore life instead of destroying it. It is a fact that the violence that Christianity is suffering from has great implications for the church. The Church in Africa needs to develop an understanding of the nature of the theology of the cross to help Christians to know how to react to violence even before it occurs. The author wants to encourage Christians to practice the right approach when responding to religious violence. This is not just an important missiological or theological response, but more importantly, it gives Christians the right intellectual and practical tools with which to face and respond to the challenges of religious violence posed to Christianity whether in Northern Nigeria, or elsewhere.

Before writing, the author spent his life in northern and central Nigeria, the same place of which Boer writes that, "bloody religious violence has continued unabated in Northern Nigeria for several decades."[1] Best also writes

> For nearly forty years the northern ruling elite gave preferential treatment to Muslims and discriminated against Christians and upsurges in the occurrences of religious violence across Northern Nigeria.[2]

During these years, one despairingly wondered why some Christians violently retaliated to religious violence. For, at the beginning of the

---

[1] Boer, Jan H. *Nigeria's Decades of Blood: Studies in Christian-Muslim Relations* (Jos, Nigeria: Stream Christian Publishers, 2003), 34.

[2] Best, Shedrack Gaya. *Conflicts and Peace Building in Plateau State, Nigeria* (Ibadan, Nigeria: Spectrum Books Limited, 2007), 3.

religious violence, Christians in Northern Nigeria appeared to have taken pacifist positions by promoting peaceful and prayerful responses to religious violence.

This book is an expression of the author's desire to help Nigerian Christians with a better approach and response to religious violence. It will also contribute to global missiology and suggest a wider theological response to violence as it encourages the general body of believers everywhere in the world. The author believes that a book such as this will greatly strengthen churches and individual believers as they seek to live for Christ in turbulent times. Like other Christian leaders, the author struggled with the problem of religious violence and its hindrances to peaceful co-existence. Yet in the middle of the violence, some Christians exhibited considerable endurance and restraint by dying as martyrs because of their faith in Christ. Their examples encouraged others not to renounce their faith, but to live victoriously, despite serious threats of violence to their lives.

Yet, there is still scope for the church to learn to listen and respond appropriately to the cries of those who are suffering violence, are discouraged and are wondering if the Divine is really in control of the situation. There is nothing as disheartening as to observe that religious violence often seems to cause spiritual disaster in many congregations. This should be deeply worrying for any reasonable leadership. On the one hand, Church history teaches that the blood of martyrs is the seed of the gospel. On the other hand, however, martyrdom might not always serve as the seed of the gospel, but may rather spell its decline and the demise of church growth. Calvin Shenk writes in his article of how churches became extinct in North Africa and Nubia.[3] For

---

[3]Shenk, Calvin. "The Demise of the Church in North Africa and Nubia and Its Survival in Egypt and Ethiopia: A Question of Contextualization?" *Missiology: An International Review*, Vol.2, April, 1993(133-154)

decades, people right across Nigeria have been living under constant threat of religious violence and are confused on how to respond. This book has been carefully crafted with the hope that the principles or guidelines and recommendations identified might help people who are experiencing religious violence.

ACKNOWLEDGEMENTS

I remain grateful to God for His unmerited grace, love, and salvation upon me and for providing men and women with the various resources and professional skills I needed to complete the Doctor of Philosophy degree studies at Concordia Theological Seminary, Fort Wayne, Indiana USA. Although the journey of my academic pursuit has been characterized by many challenges, God has been faithful. I want to thank God and the people who surrounded me with consistent prayers and financial support. It has been through their continuous and unshakable support that it was possible for me to translate my dream into reality. I find it very hard to thank everyone by name for their support throughout this study program.

This book, which has developed out of my doctoral studies, would have not been completed without the help of my supervisor and adviser, Professor Klaus Detlev Schulz, Dean of Graduate Studies and program supervisor. I am grateful for his great wealth of experience and ability to provide sound holistic theological education and godly leadership as he directs the affairs of the doctoral program. Indeed, he is an exceptional teacher, mentor and counselor. He provided encouragement and inspirational motivation throughout my studies at Concordia Theological Seminary.

My deepest appreciation goes to Cynthia Johnson, Administrative Assistant to Graduate Studies and Chapel programs, for her godly treatment towards students in the PhD program. She is such a wonderful counselor, caring, compassionate, and full of God's love in her life. Thank you for the caring and holistic services you rendered to me. This provided an enabling learning environment that sustained me to the end of my study.

I am most grateful to my writing father, Dr. John Nordling, a diligent scholar in classics and notable author, whose objective and constructive advice, guidance and encouragement has made this book a scholarly one.

I am very grateful to Northridge Baptist Church, Cook Road, Fort Wayne, Immanuel World Outreach, Illinois, and Evangelical Church, Chicago for their support.

I sincerely appreciate all the pastors and elders of ECWA Churches for being part of my success: Wuse II, Abuja; Maitama, Abuja; Appa, Lagos; Good News Church, Lafia; and Unity Church Gut-Rayfield, Jos. I am grateful to the leaders of Garki DCC for their support. My deepest thanks go to my family for their understanding, support, patience and endurance. I thank all of them for their unending love, care, and spiritual virtue that impacted my life throughout our fruitful years of fruitful relationship.

I thank all our handsome sons and beautiful daughters God has blessed us with. Alex and Lengnan, our sons are deeply appreciated for using every opportunity to pray for me and to assist me with errands when I needed it. My appreciation equally goes to our daughters; Patience, Mercy, Nandi and Keziah for giving their time to assist me in different ways.

I want to further appreciate Mr. Alex and Nanep Ladan for the sacrificial financial support they gave. I thank my sisters and brothers for their support. I want to deeply express my profound gratitude to Rev. Silas and wife Binta Dauji for the tremendous help and other services they rendered. I thank all other Nigerian Christian families that were willing to partner with me during the stress of studying and writing.

I appreciate the effort of Dr. Paul Todd, the Director of Publishing at ACTS International for taking time to edit this work.

Abbreviations

CAN	Christian Association of Nigeria
COCIN	Church of Christ in Nations Formerly Church of Christ in Nigeria
CRK	Christian Religious Knowledge
ECWA	Evangelical Church Winning All, Formerly Evangelical Churches of West Africa
FCS	Fellowship Christian Student
NLFA	New Life for All
O.I.C.	Organization of Islamic Conference
SIM	Sudan Interior Mission (now known as Serving in Mission)
TEKAN	Tarayyar Ekklisiyar Kristi a Nigeria (Fellowship of Churches of Christ in Nigeria)

CHAPTER 1

RELIGION AND VIOLENCE

Since the early 1980s, Jos Nigeria has become a classic example of multifaceted violence in Northern Nigeria. In particular, an almost unthinkable scale of mayhem and death shattered Jos' normally peaceful atmosphere as hundreds were killed in September 2001. Keith E. Eitel wrote, "Some outside reporting characterized the debacle as 'religious violence.'"[1] Jan Boer gives an account in his book, *Nigeria's Decades of Blood: Studies in Christian Muslim Relations*,[2] of a group of Muslims who took it upon themselves to stop cars along major roads in Northern Nigeria during the 2001 religious crises, and force their

------

[1] Eitel, Keith E. ed. *Missions in Contexts of Violence: Evangelical Society Series Book 15* (Pasadena: William Carey Library, 2008)25.

[2] Boer, Jan H. served for 30 years in Nigeria during which time he observed and experienced very closely the interplay between Christians and Muslims. He developed a series on Christian-Muslim relations: *Nigeria's Decades of Blood* (1980-2003), Volume 1, (Belleville, Ontario, Canada: Essence Publishers, 2003), *Muslims: Why the Violence?*, Volume 2, (Canada: Essence Publishers, 2004 *Christians: Why this Muslim Violence?*, Volume 3, *Muslims: Why We Reject Secularism*, Volume 4, *Christians: Secularism-Yes and No*, Volume 5, *Muslims: Why Muslim Sharia Law*, Volume 6, *Christians: Why we Reject Muslim Law*, Volume 7, *Christians and Muslims: Parameters for Living Together*, Volume 8).

passengers to recite the *Shahada* Islamic Creed.[3] Those passengers, who were unable or unwilling to recite the *Shahada*, were beaten or killed.[4]

The principle of an "eye for an eye" appears to be a regular method of responding to violence as Nigerian Christians abandon "cheek-turning," arguing they have no more cheeks to turn.[5] A fringe Christian militia emerged vowing to match blood for more blood and some pastors' approval of the self-defense response to violence has spiraled into angrier retaliations that have continued to fuel revenge and death over the past twenty-five years.[6]

Scott Appleby, writes,

> While religious wars seemed at one point to be a thing of the past, history has shown that violence related to religion is instead increasing both in quality and in vehemence.[7]

He further wrote, "Violence has been inflamed by religious motivations among Christians and Muslims…"[8] Thus, today, religion

---

[3] The *Shahada* is the Arabic version of Muslim profession of faith. "There is no god but Allah, and Mohammed is the prophet of Allah." The *Shahada* is the first of the five pillars of Islam. Every Muslim must recite it at least once in a lifetime, aloud, correctly, and purposively with a full understanding of its meaning and with an assent of the heart.

[4] Minchakpu, Obed is an independent journalist, who previously served as the editor of *Today's Challenge*. "Eye for an Eye: Christians Avenge February Murder, Spark Muslim Retaliation," in *Christianity Today*, 48, no. 7 July (2004): 17. Richard Nyberg, "Pastors Killed, Churches Burned: new wave of Violence Begins," *Christianity Today*, 48, no, 6 June (2004):17.

[5] Oguntola, Sunday. "No More Cheeks to Turn: Nigerian Christians Abandon Check-Turning," Christianity Today 55, no. 12 (2011): 14.

[6] Ibid.

[7] See Appleby R. Scott, *The Ambivalence of the Sacred: Religion, Violence and Reconciliation* (Boston: Rowman & Littlefield, 2000), Lee Griffith. *The War on Terrorism and the Terror of God* (Grand Rapids, Michigan: Eerdmans, 2002), Mark Juergensmeyer. *Terror in the Mind of God: The Global Rise of Religious violence* (Berkeley: University of California Press, 2001).

[8] Ibid.

in modern Nigeria is divided between a Christian culture and a radical Islamic culture. Since the September 2001 riots, different instances of religiously-related violence have continued to occur in Northern Nigeria. Each phenomenon builds on the unresolved issues of previous outbreaks resulting in the deaths of thousands. [9]

Repeatedly churches, mosques, hotels, shops, petrol stations, individual homes, and lives have been destroyed causing tremendous financial hardship on the usually uninsured owners.[10] Many have been injured, and hundreds more carry emotional scars, which hardly heal as almost annually another round of bloodshed results in fresh losses. Religious violence between Muslims and Christians characterize Northern Nigeria. This has raised the question of how the relationship between religions and violence has shown how important it is for one to think about it. One wonders what has propelled this violence in these major religions? One wonders if religion promotes violence and if it offers any resources for hindering peaceful coexistence? Christians who once advocated for pacifism speak of "no more cheeks left to turn."[11] Oguntola believes that the shift from pacifism towards self-defence developed as a result of the Kafanchan and Kaduna religious violence which began in March 1986. He notes that Christians in central Nigeria and in Northern cities mobilized to defend themselves, organizing vigilante groups to respond to terrorist attacks.[12] Aaron Frank asks,

---

[9]Gofwen, *Religious Conflicts in Northern Nigeria and Nation Building*, 1, 82-119.
[10]Ibid., 88.
[11]Ibid.
[12]Ibid.

> What is the central intellectual heresy in every faith that values
> death over life and allows otherwise decent people to turn into
> salivating storming killers in the name of religion or God?[13]

Christians need to develop their understanding on why such violence occurs and how Christians can respond to this.

The church needs to address this problem if she wants to continue to be salt and light in the world in which she lives as a witness (Matthew 5:16). "The church is the focal point of Christian faith; the study of whose doctrine is referred to as ecclesiology."[14] The Greek word for church designates a local congregation; the English word "church" being derived from the Greek *Kyriakos* meaning "the Lord's house."[15] Further, the Church could be rightly seen as the Body of the Lord Jesus Christ made up of different believers and churches grouped in one whole.[16] In today's meaning, the term "church" is often used collectively to refer to denominations such as the Evangelical Church Winning All (ECWA).[17]

Jacobsen writes that Christianity was born in the Middle East and Jerusalem was the headquarters of the movement, but the new faith quickly spread beyond Palestine.[18] From there, Christianity spread into Africa and Asia: "It was in Africa before Europe, it was in India before

---

[13]Aaron Frank and the author were travelling from Kaduna to Ilorin on February 21, 2001. It was on a day one of the major religious riots broke out in Kaduna.

[14]Gutip, Nanwul. *Church of Christ in Nations: COCIN Birth and Growth Revised Edition* (Jos, Nigeria: Cocin Printing Press, 2017), 51.

[15]Ibid.

[16]Ibid.

[17]ECWA was formerly called the Association of the Evangelical Churches of West Africa. The name was changed at the ECWA General Church Council meeting (GCC) of April 2010 when the Constitution of ECWA was amended.

[18]Jacobsen, Douglas. *The World's Christians* (United Kingdom: Wiley-Blackwell, 2007), 67.

England, and it was in China before America."[19] Walls notes that, "at the end of the twentieth century, Africa was appearing as the Christian heartland."[20] He says,

> Growth is not just a transplant from the west, but the development of an authentic African religion which coincided with the retreat of Christianity in the West; has now moved to being a major component of contemporary, representative Christianity; the standard Christianity of the present age, a demonstration model of its character.[21]

Jacobsen stresses that sub-Saharan Africa has been characterized by hope, despair, and social ills leading to violence.[22]

The Problem with Violence

To begin to understand the complex nature of the intersections of religion, violence and peace in the context of Nigeria, one needs to have a working knowledge of literature in each of these fields. Furthermore, to understand the practice of religious violence for instance, without any knowledge of specific religious traditions can lead a person to an imbalanced and incomplete knowledge of the subject of religious violence. For example, William Cavanaugh argues,

> Those who discuss religion as inherently violent rarely define religion well, if at all. Even if they do, there is little proof presented as to why religions should be considered inherently

---

[19]Ibid.

[20]Walls, Andrew F. *The Cross-Cultural Process in Christian History* (Maryknoll: Orbis Books, 2002), 118.

[21]Ibid., 119.

[22]Jacobsen, *The World's Christians*, 155-157.

violent or why religions should be singled out as fatally aggressive.[23]

Conflict in the last part of twentieth century has often been focused on the Sahalian belt of countries like Sudan and Nigeria.[24] Hans Kippenberg, a German sociologist argues that, "There is no necessary link between religious beliefs and violence. Religious violence comes neither from religions nor from secular government policies."[25] "Instead, religious violence comes from tension between religious communities and governmental, legal, and economic structures intersecting with each other."[26]

Kippenburg further argues, from a sociological point of view that

> helping groups to understand that their reactions to religious communities are not responses to, but constitutive of the violence they fear can help societies better manage their internal relationships without stoking fires of hatred and violence.[27]

Hector Avalos argues that "religion is inherently violent. Religion creates the conditions for violence by creating scarcity that would not otherwise be there."[28]

---

[23]Cavanaugh, William. *The Myth of Religious Violence: Secular Ideology and the Roots of Modern Conflict* (New York: Oxford University Press, 2009), 56.

[24]Hastings, *A World History of Christianity* (Grand Rapids: William B. Eerdmans Publishing Company, 1999), 231. "The Sahalian kingdoms were a series of kingdoms or empires that were centered on the Sahel, the area of grasslands south of the Sahara. The wealth of the states came from controlling the trade routes across the desert." http://en.wikipedia.org/wiki/Sahelian_kingdoms (accessed April 28, 2014).

[25]Kippenburg, Hans. *Violence and Worship: Religious Wars in the Age of Globalization* (Stanford: Stanford University, 2011), 38.

[26]Ibid.

[27]Kippenburg, Hans. 38.

[28]Avalos, Hector. *Fighting Wars: The Origins of Religious Violence* (Aniberst, New York: Prometheus Books, 2005), 22.

> These constructed spiritual goods are not empirically
> verifiable, yet they have a hold on people. Religion creates a
> demand, through scarcity of supply for transcendent goods that
> people are willing to kill over.[29]

Those who have experienced violence know that it is not pleasant, and would always prefer that there be no mention of violence in any given society.[30] "Violence has always been present in society and may always be so until humankind shares identical intellectual convictions."[31]

Thompson summarizes the African situation as follows: "The continent of Africa is filled with conflicts, wars from south to north, west to east, fighting burns or simmers in Africa."[32]

Violence is a problem that the church needs to address if she is to preach the gospel in a nonviolent environment. Indeed, the church in Africa has to create an understanding concerning the nature of this violence in order to respond properly to its challenges. Violence has been a serious threat to the church and at the same time a global missiological problem which has confronted Christians both in Northern Nigeria and elsewhere in the world down through history.

Origins of Violence

In the beginning, God created man and placed him in the Garden of Eden (Genesis 1: 26, 27). However, man's sin corrupted God's plan from that perfect and peaceful existence (Genesis 3: 8-14) and the perfect peace was destroyed. However, Yahweh promised hope of a future peace wherein humankind will experience the restoration of

---

[29]Ibid.

[30]Hastings laments the effect violence can have on a society. Hastings, *A World History of Christianity*, (Grand Rapids: William B. Eerdmans Publishing Company, 1999), 137.

[31]Ibid., 1247.

[32]Thompson, Milburn. *Justice and Peace: A Christian Primer* (Maryknoll: Orbis Books, 2003), 136.

peace (Genesis 3:15). God told Adam and Eve to depart from the peaceful garden into a life full of chaos (Genesis 3:23). Therefore, the life that God created for peaceful living was soon battered by violence (Genesis 4:8). From then onwards, histories of mankind became characterized by conflicts and violence. This violence continued to progress in human life until God ended the world in which Noah and the people of his own society lived (Genesis 6:11).

Old Testament Principles for Confronting Violence

In Leviticus, Kleining notes that,

> the material in 19:17-18 presupposes a tribal society made up of close blood clans, a society governed by payback. In such a society each offense had to be avenged to preserve the society's social and moral ecology.[33]

Payback operated positively as benefaction within the blood clan. It also operated negatively as revenge and hatred against those who stood outside it. The Lord, therefore, undermined the cycle of revenge by forbidding hatred and commanding love for all members of the Israelite congregation.[34] God forbade any person who had been injured to hate the offender secretly in his heart. Instead, he was required to confront the offender openly and directly with his offense. He was to rebuke his fellow Israelite to give him a chance to admit his wrongful deed and put it right.[35]

---

[33]Kleining, John W. *Concordia Commentary: A Theological Exposition of Sacred Scripture (Leviticus)* (Saint Louis: Concordia Publishing House, 2003), 412.
[34]Ibid.
[35]Ibid.

However, anybody failed to reprimand the wrongdoer, but hated him instead and plotted his downfall, that person became a party to that evil deed. Hatred of the wrongdoer turned the victim into a wrongdoer. It devoured the hateful person.[36] The offended person was therefore required to rebuke the wrongdoer or else he himself would be guilty of hatred and suffer the penalty of hatred.[37] Kleining concludes, "We are not told what the penalty was. It is, however, clear that such a person came under God's judgment."[38] The prohibition of vengeance in Leviticus19:18 follows directly from the prohibition of hatred in Leviticus19:17, for the desire for revenge and the nursing of grudges were the products of hatred.

Even if the reproof of the evildoer did not produce a positive response, the Lord did not permit his people to take revenge, or even bear a grudge against the evildoer (Leviticus 17:22). God alone paid back evildoers (Nahum 1:2; Psalm 94:1) and bore a grudge against them (Nahum 1:2; Psalm 103:9; Jeremiah 3:5, 12). These two prohibitions contradicted the most basic tenet of a tribal society, the principle of personal retaliation.

Those who had been injured could neither pay back the offender by an extra-judicial act of retribution, nor could they even indulge in secret mental scenarios of hatred and revenge.[39] All thoughts of revenge and acts of vengeance were equally forbidden. Instead, they were required to practice positive retaliation by showing love to those who had wronged them. The Israelites were required to treat those who wronged them as well as they treated themselves.[40] The love that

---

[36]Ibid.

[37]Ibid.

[38]Ibid.

[39]Kleinig, 412.

[40]Ibid.

the Lord commands is not basically an emotional attitude, a matter of sentiment, but an act of benevolence, a matter of the will, for feelings cannot be commanded.

The Lord commands his people to act in a loving way toward their neighbors and care for them as they care for themselves.[41] This commandment does not promote self-love, as if people had to love themselves before they could love others. Instead, it assumes that all people seek their own advantage, their own good, and do so without limitation or discrimination. Thus, Kleinig maintains that,

> The neighbor who was to be loved in this way was most obviously an Israelite wrongdoer. But, as shown in Leviticus 19:34, it also extended to the aliens resident with the Israelites in the land. Benevolent love was therefore to replace malevolent hatred as the response to slights and acts of injustice.[42]

All the prohibitions in this section culminate in the commandment to love the neighbor as oneself. This is the basic social duty of the Israelites as God's holy people, for God's holiness encouraged and fostered brotherly love in his congregation.[43] The kind of loving benevolence that applied to close blood relatives in a tribal society was extended to the whole congregation of Israel.

All its members were to be regarded as close spiritual kinsfolk, holy brothers and sisters in the Lord's holy family, people who all shared equally in God's holiness and who all equally came under its protection.

In the Psalms, the subject of violence is directed to questions and laments. The Psalmist raises a theological question, "Why, O, Lord, do you stand far off? Why do you hide yourself in times of trouble?"

---

[41] Ibid.

[42] Ibid., 413.

[43] Ibid.

(Psalm 10:1). Although the Psalmist recognizes God's presence, the Psalmist confidently prays that God will root out those who are wicked and take advantage of the weak and poor throughout Israel so that the wicked may not strike violence anymore (10:18). Such behavior, David reminds us, will be called to account.

There is hope, however, whether we have taken advantage of the weak or have been victim of oppression. The Lord has compassion on those oppressed by sin. The Psalmist cries to God to "break the arm of the wicked and evildoers" and eradicate violence that resonates in the world (10:15). Chilton points out that this "is part of biblical heritage at the heart of Judaism, Christianity, and Islam."[44] The teaching of nonviolence moves to the New Testament where the people of God are aliens, pilgrims, and ambassadors among the nations of the world (2 Corinthians 5:18). The Church in Jesus' time struggled with violence; the church in Nigeria as well, has been struggling with violence. John Piper wrote,

> Martyrdom is not the mere consequence of radical love and obedience; it is the keeping of an appointment set in heaven for a certain number.[45]

Wait till the number of martyrs is complete who are to be killed.[46]

---

[44]Chilton, Bruce. *Abraham's Curse: The Root of Violence in Judaism, Christianity and Islam* (New York: Doubleday, 2008), 46.

[45]Piper, John. *Filling up the Afflictions of Christ* (Wheaton, Illinois: Crossway Books, 2009), 20-21.

[46]Ibid.

CHAPTER 2

OVERVIEW OF NIGERIA

Nigeria, the most populous country in Africa with an estimated population of about 180 million is located on the Atlantic cost of West Africa, sharing borders with Benin, Niger, Chad and Cameroon. Its multi-ethnic-lingual and multi-religious society is politically divided on federal lines into 36 states with its capital in the central city of Abuja. In turn, for political reasons, the states are grouped into six geopolitical zones: South-South, South-East, South-West, North-Central, Northeast and Northwest.[1] In the Northern Region the former British colonial authorities, following a policy of Indirect Rule, retained the pre-colonial Hausa-Fulani Muslim feudal rulers and allowed them to extend their rule over the non-Muslim peoples of the Middle Belt.[2]

The majority of Nigerian Christian churches came into being through the work of Western missionaries. In the early twentieth century, these pioneers contextualized the message of the Gospel in ways that were built on traditional African worldviews. This approach,

---

[1]Appiah, Kwame Anthony and Henry Louis Gates. *Africana: The Encyclopedia of the African and African American Experience* (New York: Basic Civitas Books, 1999), 1432.

[2]Ibid., 493.

coupled with the missionaries' use of the vernacular in the adoption of (vernacular) names for God and in translation of the Scriptures, has enabled Christianity to develop deep roots in the culture and traditions of the people.

This contextual approach brought recognition that the God the missionaries proclaimed was not an alien import. Contextualisation, however, wasn't merely a technique used in the early twentieth century. For instance, in the 1970s,[3] Phil Parshall was a missionary in a South Asian Muslim country. Parshall and his team hoped to reach more Muslims by removing western cultural impediments to the gospel, since the gospel is transcultural. They tried to create identifiable Christ-centered communities using religious language (such as "Allah" for God) and cultural and religious forms (such as kneeling, Muslim style, in prayer) permitted by the Bible. However, the converts were not encouraged to remain a part of the local Islamic mosque or to call themselves Muslims. Missionaries proceeded to adopt local vocabulary to preach the gospel and pointed them to the right knowledge of the Creator. Contextualisation is also an approach rooted in the Scriptures. Thus the Apostle Paul used the symbol dedicated to the "unknown God" to point the Athenian Greeks to God (Acts 17:23, 31).

For man is created in the image of God. He is singled out for greatness above the animals (Psalm 8). The Christian's approach to the gospel, therefore, must conform to what Scripture teaches. This has implications for the African believer's worldview, whether it is related to the supernatural world, the style and message of the Christian church, or behavior towards the Scripture.

> While Islam conquered a large part of the North by force, many
> non-Muslim groups successfully resisted the war, repelled the

---

[3]Guthrie, Stan. *Missions in the Third Millennium: 21 Key Trends for the 21st Century* (Carlisle, Cumbria: Paternoster Press, 2000), 107-109.

warriors, and to a large extent embraced Christianity. Most of the groups in the North Central zone fall in this category.[4]

However, if the history is left at this point, it may not give us the necessary understanding about the early history of the Hausa states were conquered by a particular religious group.

Early Hausa States

Anthony points out that the best evidence of early civilization in Northern Nigeria is provided by the Nok terracotta heads, which are named after a village located among the Jaba people in Kwoi, in Northern Nigeria.[5] While little is known of them, we do know more and have greater understanding of the impact of the groups that established some of the largest and most enduring city-states in what is now Northern Nigeria - the Hausa states. The economic and cultural life of the early Hausa states was deeply shaped by trade. They were village-dwelling cultivators, artisans, weavers, dyers, smiths, and leather workers who produced goods for local markets as well as long distance caravans living on the belt of open woodland and grass savannah known as the Sahel, on the Southern edge of the Sahara.[6] From the southern-forested regions, these caravans brought ivory, gold, and slaves. From the north, they brought desert salt and other goods from the Mediterranean area since around the ninth century.[7] The rise of Hausa statehood coincided with the building of walled cities known as "birane."[8] The kings who resided within the cities were

---

[4]Ibid.

[5]Appiah and Gates, *Africana: The Encyclopedia of the African and African American Experience*, 1432.

[6]Ibid.

[7]Ibid.

[8]"Birane" in the Hausa language means "cities" in English.

responsible for warding off external aggression in return for which they collected taxes from commoners.[9]

It was only after the thirteenth century (AD), that the Hausa rulers began to convert to Islam and in the centuries following, cities such as Kano and Katsina became centers for Islamic scholarship as well as commerce.[10]

Many Hausa commoners were little affected by Islamic culture until the early nineteenth century (AD) when a jihad, or crusade, led by the Fulani cleric Usman Dan Fodio created a vast Islamic empire with its headquarters in Sokoto.[11] We now look at how these Hausa states were conquered.

Hausa States Conquered

Oyewole writes on how the Hausa states were conquered. Triggered in 1804 by the attempts of King Yunfa of Gobir to stem the cleric's popularity, the Jihad defeated most of the Hausa Kings by 1810,[12] putting Usman Dan Fodio and later his son Mohammad Bello in control of the largest state [now most of Northern Nigeria] during the nineteenth century, spanning some 400,000 square kilometers (154,440 square miles).[13]

Dan Fodio installed Muslim Fulani emirs in all the cities he conquered in Northern Nigeria, although he was unable to conquer what are now southern Kaduna, Jos, Plateau, and Benue states.[14] Sundita believes that religious people [like Usman Dan Fodio] sought to establish the path to the origins of their belief [Islam] as a "revival or

---

[9]Ibid.

[10]Ibid.

[11]Ibid., 1433.

[12]Ibid.

[13]Ibid.

[14]Ibid.

fundamentalism."[15] They did this with the hope of connecting to the source of their ideology,

> Whenever Muslims retrace their path to Muhammad, the result has always been to pick up the sword against the infidel because Islam prospered on violence and therefore will never go past that.[16]

> The actions of Muhammad and his immediate followers clearly demonstrate that unprovoked violence, terror, intolerance, deceit, murder, hypocrisy, and pillage continually were employed as instruments of control.[17]

The Northern Empire under Islamic control lasted for one hundred years until 1903, when Lord Lugard conquered the empire and brought it under British colonial rule.[18] The colonial officials were far more interested in business opportunities than in religious conversion and did not want Christian missionary work to interfere with their business agenda.[19] Stanley writes that, "British colonial policy in Northern Nigeria seemed actively to favor Islam and [more] to advance the cause of Islam than the Gospel of Christ."[20] Isichei records that the British colonial officials "discriminated against Christian missionaries in Northern Nigeria."[21] Miller argued, "While Muslim missionaries

---

[15]Sundiata, Abbas. *Look behind the Facade: Some Serious Stuff You're Not Supposed to Know about Islam* (USA: Xulon Press, 2006), 15.

[16]Ibid.

[17]Ibid., Sundiata, Abbas, 64.

[18]Oyewole, *Historical Dictionary of Nigeria*, 148-173.

[19]Jacobsen, *The World's Christians*, 161.

[20]Stanley, Brian. *The Bible and Flag: Protestant Missions & British Imperialism in the Nineteenth and Twentieth Centuries* (England: Apollos, Intervarsity Press, 1990), 135.

[21]Isichei, Elizabeth. *A History of Christianity in Africa: From Antiquity to the Present* (Grand Rapids: African World Press and William B. Eerdmans Publishing Company, 1995), 273.

were allowed to go anywhere under the British administration, Christian missionaries were restricted."[22] Thus, Faught argues that the emirs of Northern Nigeria were very interested in Lord Lugard and his policy of religious neutrality, which was decreed to promote their sustained cooperation.[23]

Crampton highlights a number of occasions when Christians referred to their fears of religious violence and discrimination in the North by the Muslim majority.[24] Osaghae and Suberu argue

> this transition did not accept the Christian churches either. The nature of violence in Nigeria is reported to be religious violence between Christians and Muslims and the country can rightly be described as one of the most deeply divided states in Africa.[25]

---

[22]Walls, Andrew F. *The Cross-Cultural Process in Christian History*, 151.

[23]Faught, C.B. "Missionaries, Indirect Rule and the Changing Mandate of Mission in Colonial Northern Nigeria: The Case of Canada's Rowland Victor Bingham and the Sudan Interior Mission," *Journal of Canadian Church Historical Society* 43, no. 2 (2001): 160.

[24]Crampton, Edmund P. T. *Christianity in Northern Nigeria*, 84.

[25]Osaghae E.E. and R. T. Suberu. *A History of Identities, Violence and Stability in Nigeria*, (Ibadan: Center for Research and Inequality, 2003), 4.

CHAPTER 3

MISSION WORK IN WEST AFRICA

The light of the gospel that gave birth to a flourishing church in North Africa had gone out. Although it took many years, however, the light came once again to Africa, this time to the sub-Saharan countries. Many Africans who walked in darkness came to faith in Christ by accepting the message of salvation. They opened the door and prepared the way for many who followed their footsteps and were responsible for the spread of the gospel in Africa so, the light shone once again.

The first attempts to sow the seed of the gospel in West Africa, especially in Nigeria, were made by Portuguese traders and Catholic missionaries who came to Benin and Warri around the end of the fifteenth century. For various reasons their efforts did not bring any lasting results. Tribal wars and disease, especially malaria made it difficult for Europeans. Ruth Tucker points out, "Black Africa, known for centuries as the white man's graveyard, claimed the lives of more missionaries than any other area of the world."[1] Traditional religion and culture dominated the lives of the people. While a few priests

---

[1]Tucker, Ruth A. *From Jerusalem to Irian Jaya: A Biographical History of Christian Missions* (Grand Rapids: Zondervan Publishing House, 1983), 139, 162.

continued to come, they did not make much of an effort to train local catechists who might have provided continuity in the work.[2]

By the middle of the nineteenth century, the modern missionary era in Nigeria was under way. Freed slaves who had become Christians while in different countries played a significant role in taking the gospel back to their home countries in various parts of West Africa. Lamin Sanneh points out that many former slaves returned to their people in the Lagos, Badagry, and Abeokuta areas. Other pioneer missionaries included Thomas Birch Freeman a Methodist missionary who was born in England, the son of an English mother and an African father He had already spent many years as a missionary in the Asante Kingdom, now a part of Ghana, before arriving in Lagos on September 24, 1842.[3] During this time, he also travelled to Dahomey [Benin], and the Yoruba land in Nigeria to try to establish churches in those lands.[4] Henry Townsend, from the Church Missionary Society (CMS), soon joined him on December 17 of that same year.[5]

Samuel Ajayi Crowther was captured as a slave but was rescued and sent to Sierra Leone. It is there he became a Christian and eventually trained for the Anglican priesthood before returning to Nigeria as a missionary bishop. It was then that he established a number of mission stations, including one at Abeokuta.[6] Crowther made a significant contribution, wrote a Yoruba grammar, translated many books of the Bible into the Yoruba language, and even produced a

---

[2]Ibid.

[3]Sanneh, *Translating the Message: The Missionary Impact on Culture*, 120-122.

[4]Ibid.

[5]Gye, Sunday A. *The Birth of a Church: The Story of the Evangelical Church Winning All* (Jos: Challenge Printing Press, 2010), 1.

[6]Ibid.

primer in the Igbo language.[7] He also published journals describing his expeditions on the Niger River. Crowther eventually became the first African bishop in West Africa.[8]

In 1850, the Baptists from America began to send missionaries to this area. By the end of the nineteenth century, the Western missionary movement had made advances, taking the gospel into the interior.[9]

New mission societies came to Nigeria seeking ways to penetrate inland from the coast. The Qua Iboe Mission from Britain sent European missionaries in 1887. Since 1857, Crowther, the Anglican bishop who had died in 1891, had sought to grow congregations in the north of Nigeria.[10] He promoted cordial relationships with the Northern emirs. However, not all Anglican missionaries agreed with his methods. In particular, a new group of Anglican missionaries, known as the Sudan Party had different ideas. Crampton says, "The Sudan Party eventually truncated the work of Samuel Ajayi Crowther."[11] The missionaries expected very quick results. Brooke, their leader, had calculated that within six months, much of Northern Nigeria would be converted.[12] They failed miserably. However, the failure of the Sudan Party did not quench the ardor of people who had been led to believe that the Hausas would be the most excellent material for mass conversion to Christianity. Indeed, it was this very failure that

---

[7]Walls, Andrew F. *The Cross-Cultural Process in Christian History: Studies in the Transmission and Appropriation of Faith* (Maryknoll, Orbis Books, 2002), 143-164; see also *The Missionary Movement in Christian History*, 132-139.

[8]Ibid., 139.

[9]Ibid.

[10]Crampton, E. P. T. *Christianity in Northern Nigeria with Update by: Musa A.B. Gaiya* (Bukuru, Jos, Nigeria: ACTS, 2004, 2013), 28-29.

[11]Crampton, E.P.T. *Christianity in Northern Nigeria*, 28-29.

[12]Ibid., 121.

prompted the Sudan United Mission and the Sudan Interior Mission who sent missionaries soon after.[13]

Sudan Interior Mission in Nigeria

In the latter part of the nineteenth century, Christianity seemed literally to be on the march, redrawing its historic Mediterranean and Eurocentric map to include the far-flung territories of the British Empire.[14] North America, India, and the South Pacific by now had all experienced, to a greater or lesser degree, the impact of the King James Version of the Bible. It was in this context that missionaries of the Sudan Interior Mission (SIM) contributed to planting the Christian church in Nigeria.[15]

By the 1890s, Africa was also a target of the missionary imperative characteristic of earnest late-Victorian Christianity.[16] The Sudan Interior Mission was formed in the 1890s and eventually became the largest Protestant interdenominational mission in Africa.[17] In Toronto in June 1893, Rowland Bingham had met with Mrs. Margaret Gowans, a staunch Christian woman with keen missionary instincts for the spiritual needs of the Sudan. "She spread out the vast extent of those thousands of miles south of the Great Sahara," Bingham recounted. Her passion convinced Bingham to join Mrs Gowans' son Walter in England in seeking support to evangelise in the Sudan. Along the way Thomas Kent, a college friend of Walter's, joined them. However,

---

[13]Ibid.

[14]Faught. "Missionaries, Indirect Rule and the Changing Mandate of Mission in Colonial Northern Nigeria," 147-169.

[15]Ibid.

[16]Ibid.

[17]Tucker, Ruth A. "Rowland Bingham and the Sudan Interior Mission" in *From Jerusalem to Irian Jaya: A Biographical History of Christian Missions* (Grand Rapids,: Academie Books, 1983), 295-299.

when Bingham, Gowans, and Kent landed on the coast at Lagos, they were met with a discouraging message from the Superintendent of the Methodist Mission in West Africa, saying, "Young men, you will never see the Sudan, your children will never see the Sudan, your grandchildren may."[18] The pessimistic statement could very easily have proved accurate. Yusufu Turaki wrote,

> The first decade 1893-1900, the period was the beginning of SIM. It was the formative period of the mission when several unsuccessful attempts were made to gain a foothold in the Sudan.[19]

Turaki further wrote that in

> 1893, the first attempt by the SIM's three pioneers, namely; Walter Gowans, Thomas Kent and Rowland Bingham to gain a foothold on African soil ended in dismal failure.[20]

The attempt claimed the lives of Thomas Kent (in Bida) and Walter Gowans (in Girku) and forced Bingham to make a disappointing and humiliating return to Canada.[21]

For the second attempt, 1899-1900, Bingham and his backers adopted the name African Industrial Mission believing that developing businesses would help to finance the mission as well as open the doors for evangelism. Between February and March of 1899, the mission decided to send out two missionaries, first to British East Africa, and

---

[18]The term "Sudan" at that time did not refer to the current Sudan or South Sudan but literally meant "the land of the blacks" and geographically referred to.

[19]Turaki, Yusufu. *Theory and Practice of Christian Missions in Africa: A Century of SIM/ECWA History And Legacy in Nigeria 1893-1993 Volume One*,(Nairobi, Kenya: IBS, 1999), 176.

[20]Turaki, 176.

[21]Ibid.

then to Tripoli, North Africa and finally to the Sudan.[22] This too failed with Bingham being invalided home and his colleagues following shortly afterwards.

For the third attempt, they returned to the original name of Sudan Interior Mission and sent out a party of four, namely Alex W. Banfield, E. Anthony, Albert Taylor and Charles Robinson.[23] Pategi in Nupeland was openedin March 1902 as their first missionary station.[24] This area was predominantly Muslim and quite resistant to the Gospel.[25]

Restriction of Missionaries' Efforts in Northern Nigeria

In general, colonial attitudes towards missionaries in Northern Nigeria were unfavourable. Barnes argues that up until the late 1920s colonial officials opposed most missionaries for several reasons, including:

1. They objected to the impact of evangelism;
2. Most missionaries were considered as ill-educated, unprofessional, unsuccessful, and the Americans among them were viewed as fundamentalists and fanatical;[26]
3. They lacked social graces, common sense, self-discipline, and they had entirely different goals leading to conflicts between the missionaries and the British government.[27]

---

[22]Turaki, 112.

[23]Ibid., 177.

[24]Ibid.

[25]Ibid.

[26]Barnes, A. E. "Evangelization Where It Was Not Wanted: Colonial Administrators and Missionaries in Northern Nigeria During the First Third of Nineteenth Century," *Journal of Religion in Africa*, 25 no. 4 (1995): 412-441.

[27]Crampton, *Christianity in Northern Nigeria*, 59-60.

As the largest missionary society in Northern Nigeria, SIM was intimately involved in the struggle with the colonial authorities for entrance into the Muslim emirates. Relationships with the colonial government remained difficult. Missionaries were forbidden to preach in market places or near mosques. They were not allowed to do house-to-house visitation. Evangelistic work with children and youth was a point of contention, especially in the leprosaria that missions ran across Northern Nigeria.

Beacham wrote that

> Agitation to prohibit the teaching of children under eighteen of Muslim parents, whether or not the parents desire their children to attend a Christian school or church service, has been a hindrance to advancement of the gospel in some places.[28]

Ubah refers to a 1951 plea by the Emir of Gwandu not to proselytize school children in leprosaria:

> That such a plea was made more than ten years after the matter was first raised suggests that the freedom of missionaries had not been effectively circumscribed.[29]

Because of the restrictions and discrimination against the missionaries, and fearing that with independence the situation would worsen, in the early 1950s SIM created the Evangelical Churches of West Africa [now Evangelical Church Winning All] (ECWA) denomination out of the various SIM Churches already existing.[30] (The Church has grown in numbers since it was incorporated in a 1954 registration with the

---

[28]Beacham, C.G. *Annual Field Report for Nigeria and French West Africa 1940*, Soul Winning, April (1941), Vol. 17, No. 2: 1-14.
[29]Ubah, *Colonial Administration and the Spread of Islam in Northern Nigeria*, 13.
[30]Musa, Danladi. *Strategic Plan 2007-2016* (May 2007), 1-156.

Federal Government of Nigeria. It currently estimates its membership to be over six million).[31]

However, the absence of religious freedom continued even after the ECWA was formed in 1954.[32] The aim had been to allow the church to inherit the property of the founding missionaries and continue the work in case the mission was expelled from Nigeria, perhaps after independence in 1960.[33] SIM missionaries were afraid that the example of missionaries being expelled from China would be repeated in Nigeria. It was a very worrying possibility. Fuller quoted Ray Davis saying that the new church faced impossible odds. "History and culture were against her. One of those opponents was Islam, and its discrimination against Christians and traditionalists."[34]

The absence of religious freedom concerned delegates attending the 1956 ECWA General Assembly. They felt that the inclusion of a human rights clause in the Federal Constitution would provide legal safeguards. Sir Ahmadu Bello, the Premier of Northern Nigeria, was invited to address a joint ECWA/SIM meeting in Jos where he assured them there would be no interference in mission work although Muslims would not be encouraged to convert to Christianity.[35]

Nevertheless, churches were still concerned about the religious freedom of their new converts in Northern Nigeria. The situation compelled the Anglican, TEKAN, and ECWA denominations to produce a joint statement to the Willinks Commission hearing in

---

[31]Musa, *Strategic Plan 2007-2016*, 156.

[32]David I. Olatayo, *ECWA: The Root, Birth and Growth Book 1* (Ilorin, Nigeria: Ocare Publications, 1993), 1-48.

[33]Ibid., 21.

[34]Harold W. Fuller, *Mission-Church Dynamics* (Pasadena: William Carey Library, 1980), 199.

[35]Olatayo, *op. cit.*, 39-41.

Zaria[36], calling for guarantees of fair representation, equality under the law, religious liberty, and equal rights to education, employment and promotion.[37] These church denominations did not make any representation regarding state creation (such as agitation for a Middle Belt State): instead, they sought constitutional guarantees.[38] These requests were granted in 1959 when a Human Rights Declaration for the Northern Region was promulgated.[39]

However, the rights and freedom of worship for Christians were still not guaranteed. Even when Nigeria got independence on October 1, 1960, some mission organizations in Northern Nigeria were apprehensive. They feared persecution and the continuous absence of religious liberty for the churches they planted. An example was the Lutheran missionaries, Kastfelt writes that

> Danish Lutherans and their converts in Numan and Yola observed that the mood of missionaries was very uncertain. Various questions were raised. What would happen with their schools and mission stations? How would it face the challenges of nationalism and Islam?[40]

To meet these challenges, the Danish Lutheran missionaries redoubled their evangelism, and developed their leadership training both for

---

[36]N., Bagudu. (ed.) *Proceedings at the Sir Henry Willinks Commission Appointed to Enquire into the Fears of the Minorities and Means of Allaying Them, Volume 1* (Jos: League for Human Rights, 2003), 220-238.

[37]Bagudu, *Proceedings at the Sir Henry Willinks Commission Appointed to Enquire into the Fears of the Minorities and Means of Allaying Them*, 220-238.

[38]Ibid.

[39]Olatayo, *ECWA: The Root, Birth and Growth Book 1*, 42-43.

[40]Kastfelt, Niels. *Religion and Politics in Nigeria: A Study in Middle Belt Christianity* (London: British Academic Press, 1994), 36-38.

church purposes, and to provide the secular leaders the country would need.[41]

When it came to ECWA, Olatayo writes that there continued to be outstanding cases of violence against ECWA members and denial of human rights,

> As a body and as individuals, members were denied rights which were granted to other citizens: rights to parcels of land to locate and build church property and buildings respectively; denied freedom of proclamation of one's faith and so forth.[42]

In part, these tensions arose from the active promotion of Islam by Sir Ahmadu Bello, the Premier of Northern Nigeria. However, Olatayo writes that the 1966 ECWA General Church Council heard reports of threats to burn a church in a particular village if it held services while Sir Ahmadu Bello campaigned there. However, Sir Ahmadu Bello could not get to the village, as "God intervened by sending out fire from His presence, the fire burnt up his car on the way to the village."[43] Since then, Christian response to religious violence has become complex. This becomes necessary for us to understand religious violence in the next chapter.

---

[41]Kastfelt, *Religion and Politics in Nigeria*, 38.

[42]Olatayo, *The Roots, Birth and Growth Book 2*, 33-34, 53, 55.

[43]Olatayo, *The Roots, Birth and Growth Book 2*, 33-34, 53, 55.

CHAPTER 4

UNDERSTANDING RELIGIOUS VIOLENCE

The unforgettable Dogo Nahawa[1] experience can serve as an example for understanding religious violence. Violence occurred in the wake of April 2009 when fanatical Fulani herdsmen descended on an entire Christian community in Dogo Nahawa town in Jos South local government, Plateau State, Nigeria. It was a terrible night and a ghastly sight to behold the next day. The entire Christian community was taken by surprise. Their houses were burnt down. Men, women and children were ambushed and slaughtered like animals. Today, the violence has left Dogo Nahawa orphans in perpetual pain tormented by the horrible fate meted on their parents.

Two words, *khamas* and *shodh* are used in Hebrew to render the English word "violence." In English, violence carries the meaning of,

> Using physical force so as to injure, damage, roughness in action and negatively as the use of force, or power, as in

---

[1]My wife and our last daughter partnered in 2016 with Jordan Eye Hospital, Jos on a medical outreach to the orphans and a few women in Dogo Nahawa. My daughter reported that, "the place is like a ghost town full of graves." She wondered what story would these orphans tell their next generation concerning what happened to their parents.

> deprivation of rights, and brute strength that inflicts pain,
> injury, cruel or unjust action, with hostile intent.[2]

In a Biblical sense, violence conveys the meaning "to pursue, to oppress, or to afflict."[3] Thus, violence cannot occur unless the perpetrator actually acts out his violent inclinations. This action must be perceived as unjust and reveals itself in diverse ways. If this happens, violence occurs within a broader spectrum, and ranges from unjust actions that are intensely hostile to those that are mildly hostile.

Intensely hostile actions can be executed physically, psychologically, and or socially. These could encompass actions such as beating, discrimination, torture, and even death. Such action usually strikes at an individual's basic needs. Thus, a pastor from the northeast of Nigeria held to an extremely circumscribed view of violence denying the presence of religious violence because he had not personally seen any cases of physical brutality even though his church, under a religiously oppressive governor, was denied access to worship. That same governor had demolished many worship places in the district for which that pastor was chairman. Yet, it is not only oppression from those in authority. It is well known that in certain parts of Jos in Central Nigeria, despite the city being predominantly Christian, worshippers are forced to travel to church using complex and varying routes in order to avoid confrontation and probably death. Schlossberg maintains that similar responses are common among Christians in other regions of the world, including areas where religious freedom

---

[2]*Webster's New World College Dictionary*, Fourth Edition (New York: Macmillan, 1999), 1595.

[3]Middleton, Richard. *The New Interpreter's Dictionary of the Bible* (Nashville: Abingdon Press, 2009), 783.

may be the law, but in practice, Christians are still subject to a wide range of violence.[4]

The Merriam-Webster Collegiate Dictionary, Tenth Edition, states that violence results in "bodily harm," or "oppress cruelly," especially due to religion, politics or race.[5] However, the definition of violence by Barrett, Kurian, and Johnson underscores a theological meaning of religious violence towards Christians. These authors write that violence is

> Any unjust action of varying levels of hostility perpetrated primarily on the basis of religion and directed at Christians resulting in varying levels of harm as it is considered from the victim's perspective.[6]

This meaning of religious violence has three important elements that can further be elucidated as follows:

1. <u>Varying levels of hostility/varying levels of harm.</u> Religious violence manifests itself within a broad spectrum ranging from mildly hostile to intensely hostile actions. Mildly hostile actions are less intense and can be carried out psychologically or socially. These actions can include ridicule, restriction, certain kinds of harassment, or discrimination. Intensely hostile actions lie at the opposite end of the spectrum and can also be carried out psychologically or socially, as well as physically. In the light of this, one cannot theologically define religious violence based solely on the level of harm it might cause or level of hostility in which

---

[4]Schlossberg, Herbert. *Called to Suffer, Called to Triumph* (Portland: Multnomah Press, 1990), 17.

[5]*Merriam-Webster's Collegiate Dictionary*, Tenth Edition (Springfield: Merriam-Webster Incorporated, 1998), 1319.

[6]Barrett, David B., George T. Kurian, and Todd Johnson. *World Christian Encyclopedia* (New York: Oxford University Press, 2001), 27.

it occurs. Rather, it must be understood to encompass actions spanning the full range of hostility, from mild to intense.

2.   <u>Perpetrated primarily on the basis of religion.</u> While religious violence often occurs within the context of overlapping motivations, for example religion, race, culture, politics, and so forth, for violence to be classified as religious violence then religion must be the primary factor involved in the event. With this in mind, Marshall provides the helpful demarcation that

> If the persons had other religious beliefs, would they still be treated in the same way? If the answer is yes, we probably should not call it specifically religious violence, though not for a second should we forget that it is real violence and that it is real people who suffer.[7]

3.   <u>Victim's perspective.</u> Perhaps most important, this aspect acknowledges the fact that violent people cannot be the judges of their actions. For example, in the early parts of Acts, we see Saul violently arresting and murdering followers of Jesus Christ, because to Saul they posed a threat to the Jewish religious system. Saul's actions were surely justifiable to him in the light of how he viewed Christians and their claims. In Acts 9:1-6, however, Jesus Himself clarifies this issue for Saul saying that not only is he violating the church, but he is doing violence to Christ Himself. From the perspective of Saul's victims, his actions were unjust and violent.

Koschorke argues that when there is a situation where restrictions and violent actions against a particular religious belief are widespread and consistent, such actions are to be classified "as religious

---

[7]Marshall, Paul. "Persecution of Christians in the Contemporary World," *International Bulletin of Missionary Research 22*, no. 1 (January 1998): 2-8.

harassment and religious discrimination."[8] It is, therefore, important to distinguish religious violence from sociopolitical violence. Sociopolitical definitions in general understand religious violence to be any systematic violence of religious freedom.[9] Although the word "religious" is not readily available in the Bible motif, the concept and motif is implied throughout the biblical narrative running through the Old and New Testaments.

Violence through the Ages

The subject of violence is a general phenomenon in the history of humanity. The issue of violence runs through the times of the Maccabees. The Zealots believed there was no contradiction between prayer and the sword. Josephus writes about the Jewish sects comprising, the Pharisees, the Sadducees, the Essenes and especially, the Zealots who "could hardly resist drawing their swords."[10]

The Qumran community saw that God's coming included war between the sons of light and the sons of darkness (2 Maccabees 15:16). In its earliest history, the church passed through much bloody violence. It is surprising to observe that violence and destruction have been part and parcel of religions from biblical times.

Why does religion seem to need violence and why is a divine mandate for destruction accepted with such certainty by some believers?[11] War is normally understood mainly in terms of "armed

---

[8]Koschorke, Klaus. *A History of Christianity in Asia, Africa and Latin America, 1450-1990* (Grand Rapids: William B. Eerdmans Publishing Company, 2007), 268.

[9]Marshall, "Persecution of Christians in the Contemporary World," 19-30.

[10]Josephus, Flavius. *Josephus: The Essential Writings* Translated and Edited, Paul L. Maier (Grand Rapids, Michigan, Kregel Publications, 1988), 209,222, 317.

[11]Huntington, S.P. *The Clash of Civilizations and the Remaking of the World Order* (London: Touchstone Books, 1996), 252.

conflicts between different nations, states or groups."[12] From this understanding, the ethics of war focus on the responsibilities of citizens in time of war, non-resistance, pacifism, preventive war, and what constitutes war from nations to nations. The contrast in Africa is that war and violence are seldom international in nature. Rather, they involve two religious groups, making it best defined as religious violence. The sub-Saharan churches have been characterized by violence of all sorts; among such have been religious wars. Nevertheless, what insight can theologians, philosophers and Christian ethical writers gain concerning religious violence?

Insight on Religious Violence

Theologians, philosophers, Christian ethical writers, and their contributions provide insights for us on the subject of religious violence. Against scholars and communicators who argue religion as a cause of violence, Charles Selengut makes a case for taking religion seriously. Selengut believes that "religion is a different order and religious faith and the rules and directives of religion are characterized by social interaction."[13]

Selengut approaches religion as a social group where dynamics of leadership and membership are controlled as to how "religion is invoked to create or sustain violence."[14] Here religion is understood as theodicy, viewing religious violence through the

> civilizational perspectives, with violence as a means to protect
> a group that perceives itself as threatened, through the

---

[12]Soames, Catherine, Sara Hawker, and Julia Elliott. *Oxford Dictionary of Current English* (Oxford: Oxford University Press, 2006), 1040.

[13]Selengut, Charles. *Sacred Fury: Understanding Religious Violence*, 2nd ed.(Lanham, Maryland: Rowman & Littlefield, 2008),6.

[14]Selengut, 6.

> apocalyptic perspectives, where religious actors see violence as salvific…[15]

Thus, Paul spoke of his scars as "the mark of Jesus." In his wounds, people could see Jesus' wounds. He says in Galatians 6:17, "I bear on my body the marks of Jesus." The lesson of bearing the marks of Jesus is that Jesus might be seen and that his love might work powerfully among the pagans who see. From Paul's viewpoint violence is, therefore, not something that happens only at gunpoint. It is also present whenever the human dignity of an individual is oppressed, ignored or abused. Today, violence can be the ethos of our perilous times. It can also be the spirituality of the modern world. It can be accorded the status of a religion, demanding from its devotees an absolute obedience to death.

Piper quoted Tertullian who wrote about the violence Christians experienced: "The oftener we are mown down by you [Romans], the more in number we [Christians] grow; the blood of Christians is seed."[16] Piper wrote, "For almost three hundred years, Christianity grew in soil that was wet with the blood of the martyrs."[17]

Today, there also seems to be a growing awareness that our world desperately needs a counter ethos that affirms life, in order to create livable conditions for generations to come by applying the pacific lifestyles of our forbearers. From the pacifism of early Christianity through to the mid-twentieth century, we see that Christian principles taught that we should neither respond violently in self-defence to violence, nor seek the elimination of those who caused violence. Cahill says,

---

[15]Ibid., 11.

[16]Ibid.

[17]Ibid.

The ultimate consideration in Christian social ethics, when mortal violence is in question, is whether a preferential option is being made for justice for those least able to advance their own cause.[18]

Hauerwas puts forward the question,

How can the church be at this time a people of patience who take the time to step back in the face of terrible events?

He answers,

Christians are a community shaped by the practice of baptism that reminds us there are far worse things that can happen to us than dying.[19]

Sider believes that

God has not suspended the Biblical commands to work for the good of all (Galatians 6:10) and love your enemies (Matthew 5:44). It is crucial that the church offer a Biblical answer to the question.[20]

Clapsis wonders,

What should be the relationship of the Christian faith to the violence existing in the world and how should Christians respond to violence in a matter that is rooted in faith and their relationship to God?[21]

---

[18]Cahill, Lisa Sowle. *Strike Terror No More: Theology, Ethics and the New War*. Edited by Jon L. Berquist (Saint Louis, Missouri: Chalice Press, 2002), 230.

[19]Hauerwas, Stanley. *In Strike Terror No More: Theology, Ethics and the New War*. (Saint Louis: Chalice Press, 2002), 246.

[20]Sider, Ronald J. *How Should Christians Respond? Strike Terror No More: Theology, Ethics, and the New War*, (Saint Louis: Chalice Press, 2002), 326.

[21]Clapsis, Emmanuel. *Violence and Christian Spirituality: An Ecumenical Conversation* (Geneva: WCC Publications, 2007), 3.

Jesus's liberating message of love without restriction includes also renunciation of violence that destroys one's fellow man physically or mentally.

Jessica Stern wrote, "We engage religious terrorism on the ideological level by hold[ing] fast to the best of our principles, by emphasizing tolerance, empathy, and courage."[22] We draw insight from these writers that violence has irreparable consequences for the individual and for society. They provide perspectives on religious violence and some of these scholars have offered suggestions concerning how to respond to the question of religious violence as it impacts Christianity.

---

[22]Stern, Jessica. *Terror in the Name of God: Why Religious Militants Kill* (New York: Ecco, 2003) 296.

CHAPTER 5

HUMAN VIOLENCE IN SCRIPTURE

God's Word teaches that when the work of creation was completed, he appraised that it was very good. "God saw all that he made and it was good" (Genesis 1:31). How come that what God called "very good" finds itself in disorder, crisis, war and destruction? The Bible explains that it is the wickedness of human hearts that have led mankind to envy, strife and jealousy. The result of these wicked tendencies resulted in the first human violence. Since then the world has been dominated with suspicion, greed, jealousy, envy, robbery, violence and war. It is, therefore, human wickedness and the inclination to evil that has brought about the lack of peaceful living on earth.

Human Violence in Genesis

Very early in the Biblical narrative we read the story behind Cain's murder of his brother Abel. God favored Abel's sacrifice. God did not pay attention to Cain's offering (Genesis 4:3-5). Abel's offering was not inherently superior to Cain's. Throughout the Old Testament, God looks with just as much favor on grain and other produce offerings, as He does on animal offerings (Leviticus 1-6). Rather, God regarded Abel's offering because it was given in true faith (Hebrews 11:4). Cain, however, had made the common mistake of thinking that God can be influenced by means of our offerings (Genesis 4:6). He had forgotten that God repeatedly makes it clear that He will be gracious to whom He will be gracious, and He will show mercy upon whomever He will show mercy (Exodus 33:19). Thus, in the second generation of humanity, a brother spills the blood of his brother. Cain murdered Abel because he was jealous.

The pattern is set. If jealousy is left unchecked it will grow, deepen, and intensify, and result in violence. Those who give in to violence find sin crouching at the door, but "you must rule over it" (Genesis 4:6, 7).[1] Cain did not heed God's warning. He gave into the domination of sin and exercised his angry desire by killing his brother (Genesis 4:8). The Bible states that jealousy leads to anger and that sin is predatory, crouching at the door, looking to possess Cain. Violence, in other words, is often the tipping point after resentment turns to rage.

What can be done about violence? Cain did not heed the warning, and blood was spilled. God responds to Cain, "The voice of your brother's blood is crying to me from the ground" (Genesis 4:8). McEntire writes that this first act of violence foreshadows the wickedness and evil of all humanity, and would cause God to blot it out with the flood (Genesis 6:5-7).[2] Moreover, so does the blood of many today. The lesson on violence to learn from this biblical passage is that violence is the result of the pathology of the soul. Violence does not generate from military service, generational tribal hatred, or longstanding social inequities. Rather, violence is as close to us as our own hearts.

---

[1]Engelbrecht, Edward A. *The Study Bible, English Standard Version* (Saint Louis: Concordia Publishing House, 2009). All quotations hereafter shall be from this translation, except as otherwise noted.

[2]McEntire, Mark. *The Blood of Abel: The Violent Plot in the Hebrew Bible* (Macon: Mercer University Press, 1979), 1.

Later in Genesis, a profound principle is laid down regarding the moral depravity of violence. "Whoever sheds the blood of man by man shall his blood be shed, for God made man in His own image" (Genesis 9:6). This is also early in the Biblical account. This is foundational in the sense that it links to the foundational reality that violence against human beings is wrong because human beings are made in the image and likeness of God (Genesis 1:26, 27). There is worth and dignity in human life that should not be taken by another person.

Worth and Dignity of Human Life

There is a worth, a value, and a dignity to every human life. This understanding comes from the reality that man was created in the image of God (Genesis 1:26, 27; 2:7). In the *Concordia Self-Study Bible*, Roehrs points out,

> Man's unique status among all other creatures derives from his relationship to the Creator. It is not a physical replica of God (Isaiah 40:18; Luke 24:39; John 4:24) nor an emanation or a part of God; not independent of God.[3]

Man is given features that correspond and relate to the Creator. These include the capacity to share in His rulership and responsibility to exercise partnership in a communion with Him, reflecting how God wants him to be and act. Thus, we bear His "likeness and imprint."[4]

When man subsequently broke this divinely stipulated relationship dragging all creation with him into frustrating disharmony (Romans 8:20-23), he lost the ability to live and act in harmony with God and his fellow human beings as he was intended

---

[3]Roehrs, Walter R. *Concordia Self-Study Bible* (Saint Louis: Concordia Publishing House, 1971), 18.
[4]Ibid.

to do (Genesis 3, 5:1-3; James 3:9).[5] Capon makes some observations in his book, *Is God a Moral Monster?* He lists the following four observations:

1. Not everything that happened in the Old Testament times was condoned by God;

2. Some of the violence in the Old Testament was a protection against hostile powers and the judgment of God;

3. The nation of Israel in the Old Testament was a theocracy; and

4. It is obvious from reading the New Testament that from that point on, an entirely different set of ethics applies with the coming kingdom of God with Jesus.[6]

Dietrich wrote, "The Hebrew Scriptures are not a primer on violence, but, in a surprising fullness and diversity, offer guidance for overcoming violence."[7] He shows how Biblical passages guide the readers to hinder, limit, reject, and prevent violence, and to eliminate its causes, all the while offering the hope of an ultimate end to violence.[8] Brueggemann argues, "Yahweh is said to work violence that belongs to the enforcement of sovereignty."[9] Violence, therefore, is not part of God's creation. Violence is a result of the chaos, alienation and pride of the fallen humanity (Genesis 3: 1-14), and it will not be

---

[5]Ibid.

[6]Copan, Paul. *Is God a Moral Monster? Making Sense of the Old Testament God* (Grand Rapids: Baker Books, 2011), 20-222.

[7]Dietrich, Walter. "The Mark of Cain: Violence and Overcoming Violence in the Hebrew Bible," *Theology Digest* 52 (2005), 3-11.

[8]Dietrich, "The Mark of Cain," 3-11.

[9]Brueggemann, Walter. *Theology of the Old Testament: Testimony, Dispute, Advocacy* (Minneapolis: Fortress Press, 1997), 381.

part of the New Kingdom either.[10] Genesis 4 begins with a murder and traces how the shadow of violence lengthens until Lamech perverts God's intention for marriage by taking two wives and boasting that he is seventy-seven times more violent than his murderous ancestor Cain (4:23-24). Nevertheless, we also learn of the birth of Seth, through whom God's promise in Genesis 3:15 will continue. God's plan is not stopped by violence. God appoints another seed of the woman to receive the promise and to carry the story forward (Genesis 4:25-26). Engelbrecht concludes,

> The promise continues to unfold until it comes at last to the cross. There, Satan tries to derail God's plan by killing the seed of the woman. Once again, God prevails, not by appointing another, but by raising Jesus from the dead in declaration that the work is finished, creation is redeemed.[11]

Confession for God's Deliverance

How the believer should respond to violence is a recurrent theme in the book of Psalms. Psalm 10 is a psalm of lament which concludes with the faithful assertion of God's inevitable goodness and right action on behalf of the victims (Psalm 10:17, 18). This vision of ultimate justice is familiar to those who read the Psalms. Throughout the Psalms, the voice of Israel speaks reflecting the nation's historical experience. They protest against injustice and violence and use strong language against Babylon (Psalm 137:8, 9). Alexander notes,

---

[10]Atkinson, David J. ed., *New Dictionary of Christian Ethics and Pastoral Theology* (Leicester: InterVarsity Press, 1995), 877.
[11]Engelbrecht, *The Study Bible*, 23.

> It is the cry of Israel in the despair of exile, committing to Yahweh its strongest desire for revenge and trusting Him to do what is right.[12]

Psalms such as this one speak to the language of Israel's heart—passionate for God's glory, immersed in the pain, ambiguities and turmoil of history, and offering them all to God.[13]

By turning to God in distress and addressing Him, the petitioner shows his complete dependence on God. To look elsewhere for deliverance would be contrary to God's will. God's presence will inevitably reside with those who are most needy in order to strengthen them from within. God pays attention to the needs of the disadvantaged and the terrorized. God will perform justice for the unfortunate, the abandoned, and all victims. Perhaps an even greater testimony is that which Isaiah and other minor prophets perceived with regards to the coming end of violence.

Prophecy of a Peaceful Kingdom

These great prophetic testimonies of peace in the Bible appear to be relevant for all who have suffered violence. Isaiah presents a vivid prophetic picture of anticipated peace in which nations

> will hammer their swords into plowshares and their spears into pruning hooks. No nation will raise a sword against another or train for war anymore.
>
> —Isaiah 4:2

This theme of transforming swords into plowshares is also seen in Micah (4:3 and Joel 3:9-10). Swords and plowshares were two valuable

---

[12]Alexander, Desmond. *New Dictionary of Biblical Theology* (Downers Grove: InterVarsity Press, 2000), 834.
[13]Ibid.

uses of metal. Each could be transformed into the other, allowing people to tend the ground or kill their neighbor. The Old Testament prophets looked forward to a future Savior who would crush violence and become the "Prince of Peace" (Isaiah 9:6). Waltke comments, "Isaiah outlines this new model of holy war that is a spiritual, not political, kingdom."[14]

This was not a political, but a spiritual kingdom prophesied in Hosea 1:7, Zechariah 4:6b; and in Micah 7:18-20. The separation between political and spiritual powers comes to its full fruition in the New Testament. The Messiah does not wield a carnal sword that cuts flesh, but a sword that cuts hearts. The author of Hebrews 4:12 presents this. The Bible is not simply a collection of words from God. It is not a mere vehicle for communicating ideas. It is living and life changing and dynamic as it works in human beings to turn them from violence to life. God turns political and military power over to the state, while turning the spiritual power over to Jesus Christ who conquers the real enemy behind the world powers.

In the New Testament, the focus shifts to Jesus' teaching on revenge and his teaching on loving your neighbor. Stott writes,

> The authority of Jesus is equal to the law, but does not replace it. However, because of His authority as King and Son of God, the Law is reshaped and re-angled, so that instead of emphasizing the difference between Israel and the Gentile nations, the Law is now seen to encourage love for enemies (5:38-48) and a breaking down of the barrier between Jews and Gentiles (15:1-28).[15]

---

[14]Waltke, Bruce K. *An Old Testament Theology: An Exegetical Canonical and Thematic Approach* (Grand Rapids: Zondervan Publishing House, 2007), 402.

[15]Stott, John. *Men with a Message: An Introduction to the New Testament and Its Writers* (London: Evangelical Literature Trust, 1994), 39.

Given this universal human condition, it was inevitable that some teachers in first-century Judaism would have taken the Biblical admonitions regarding just penalties and recompense (Exodus 21:24; Leviticus 24:20; Deuteronomy 19:21) and married them. "This [is the] perspective of do what you have to, and be sure to get even."[16] Gibbs concludes, "This is as far away from the Torah's intention as the east is from the west."[17]

Kleinig summarizes how the Law's statements about retribution were intended to function, even on the level of legal interactions in non-Israelite societies where "the *lex talionis*" was already accepted in Mesopotamia long before it was mentioned in the Old Testament. The lex talionis, meaning the "eye for eye," rule was instituted as a guide for judges; not as a rule for personal relationships or to justify revenge. This rule made the punishment fit the crime, thereby preventing the cruel and barbaric punishments that characterized many ancient countries. Jesus used this principle to teach non-retaliation in (Matthew 5:38-48). In place of a spirit of grudging recompense and quick revenge, Jesus calls His disciples to be wise as serpents but harmless as doves.

Gibbs affirms Luther that

> His words are to reform our instincts, our quick reactions, and our unwillingness to sacrifice. St. Paul hits very close to this same target with his admonition to not repay evil for evil, but overcome evil with good (Romans 12:18-21).[18]

Thompson argues that

---

[16]Ibid.

[17]Ibid.

[18]Gibbs, *Concordia Commentary: A Theological Exposition of Sacred Scripture* (Matthew 1:1-11:1), 303.

> This act allows the inferior in the relationship to assert her
> or his equal humanity with the oppressor, and it forces the
> oppressor to take stock of the relationship and perhaps of the
> social system that supports such inequality. It is risky, to be
> sure, and demands courage, but it is a creative way to challenge
> an unhealthy relationship and unjust.[19]

If Jesus' disciples will err, let it be on the side of not retaliating, of yielding, of giving, or of being taken advantage of. A backhanded slap to the face is not assault.[20] Jews in the first century could readily be forced by occupying Roman soldiers to relinquish possessions or even for a time their freedom.[21]

The One who teaches these things [Himself] embodied, such willing nonresistance and self-sacrifice and quiet submission to evil men when He gave His back to blows and His cheeks to striking.[22] In the strength of eschatological blessings (5:3-12), Jesus' disciples can learn to exhibit this strong softness, gaining more by giving up what might be theirs by reasonable expectation and by right. Jesus explaining the true meaning of revenge in the law now addresses love for one's neighbor.

---

[19]Thompson, Milburn. *Justice and Peace: A Christian Primer* (Maryknoll: Orbis Books, 2003), 192.

[20]Gibbs, Jeffrey A. clarifies that commentators may be correct in supposing that a slap specifically on the right cheek (5:19) is likely a backhand slap, since most people are right-handed.

[21]Keener, Craig S. *The IVP Bible Background Commentary: New Testament* (Downers Grove: Intervarsity Press, 1993), 199, writes that Roman soldiers "could requisition what they required and legally demand local inhabitants to provide forced labor" (Matthew 27:32).

[22]Allison, Dale. "Anticipating the Passion," argues for connections between Matthew 5:38-42 and the Passion Narrative, with Isaiah 50:6 as the mediating link, after noting the verbal parallels among the texts (page 703).

Jesus' Teaching on Love
Matthew 5:43-48

The desire to limit one's loving deeds to a particular group manifests itself wherever sinners are. Jesus' teaching in Matthew 5:43-48 rejects this universal tendency, just as He did in Matthew 5:38-42. Scaer writes pointedly,

> The commands to love the enemy and pray for the persecutors are given with the express intent that they must and can be fulfilled in the community of Jesus (5:11). These are not optional. If these commands are not carried out, this community is no longer recognized as belonging to Jesus.[23]

Jesus commands His disciples to love without reference to the worthiness of the person being loved and to pray for others in the same way. Even the enemy and the persecutor must receive the loving deeds and prayers of Jesus' disciples. Gibbs says,

> Love in Biblical parlance does not refer to an emotion, but rather to an attitude of good intention that issues forth in appropriate action for the good of the other. It has nothing necessarily to do with liking someone or with emotions.[24]

His disciples' purpose in loving and praying in this way is to give the evidence that they are the sons of the heavenly Father, who is known only in Jesus (Matthew 11:27). The Father is good to both evil and good, to just and unjust. This is evident in the realm of creation, where God does not withhold His good gifts from those who have set themselves against Him in unbelief and rebellion (Romans 3:23, 6:23).

---

[23]Scaer, David P. *Sermon on the Mount: The Church's First Statement of the Gospel* (Saint Louis: Concordia Publishing House, 2000), 137-38.

[24]Gibbs, *Concordia Commentary: A Theological Exposition of Sacred Scripture* (Matthew 1:1-11:1), 306.

It is preeminently so in Jesus Himself, who gave His life as the ransom for all (Matthew 20:28).

In this literary and canonical context, Jesus' primary aim is not to condemn His disciples as the sinners that they surely are, but rather to reveal to His disciples the will of God for their calling as the salt of the earth and light of the world (Matthew 5:13-16). Their relationship with Jesus and with His Father is created by repentance (Matthew 4:17) and faith in the promised blessings that Jesus pronounced in the Beatitudes (Matthew 5:3-12). In that relationship and strengthened by that blessing, Jesus' disciples will individually, and corporately, begin to manifest the will of God for their lives. They know all the while that their quest for perfection has nothing to do with causing or maintaining their standing in the presence of God. Jesus the Lord is the one who manifests absolute perfection on behalf of His disciples, and His completed work for them is at all times the certain hope and confidence of His disciples (Matthew 5:19).

Sell Your Garment and Buy a Sword
Luke 22:35-38

Jesus' final words to the disciples seem to reverse the instructions He gave in Luke 9:1-6 and 10:1-12 when He sent the Twelve and the seventy-two respectively to preach the kingdom of God and to heal. Just writes,

> Then He sent them without provisions so they would have to depend on God to sustain them through the gifts offered by their host families, much as a pastor is supported by his congregation (cf 10:6).[25]

---

[25]Just, Arthur A. *Concordia Commentary: A Theological Exposition of Sacred Scripture* (Luke 9:51-24:53) (Saint Louis: Concordia Publishing House, 1997), 851.

Is Jesus changing His mind? Is He instituting a new pattern for mission? Why does Jesus not instruct His disciples to provide for themselves and even arm themselves for violent conflict by selling their garments and buying swords? In Acts, the disciples held everything in common, renouncing their individual possessions (Acts 2-4). They willingly endured persecution and offered no armed resistance (Acts 5, 7, 8,12,16,17, and 19). Hengel believes that Jesus' teaching of nonviolence demanded of His followers that they renounce violence and love their enemies.[26] However, it may be inferred that Jesus had taken no exception to them bearing the ordinary means of self-defense when traveling in bandit-infested country beyond the protection of armed authority.[27]

Keener comments, "Protecting Jesus was a paramount issue, yet Jesus did not want His disciples to protect him (see also 5:44)."[28] Keener believes,

> For Matthew, Jesus came to conquer by way of suffering on the cross, not by way of wielding the sword. Yet, it is easier in human terms, for disciples to fight for their cause than simply to embrace martyrdom for it without resistance; once they realized that martyrdom without resistance was the price for following Jesus, the disciples fled.[29]

Jesus had already plainly affirmed that in the process of fulfilling His mission, He would die a violent death. It was not appropriate for the disciples to attempt to prevent this. Keener further comments,

---

[26]Hengel, Martin. *Victory over Violence: Jesus and Revolutionists* (Philadelphia: Fortress Press, 1973), 88.

[27]Ibid., 23.

[28]Keener, Craig S. *A Commentary on the Gospel of Matthew* (Grand Rapids: William B. Eerdmans Publishing Company, 1999), 642.

[29]Ibid.

"They came prepared for armed resistance from one they supposed was a messianic revolutionary. These are not the words of a violent revolutionary (26:47)."[30]

Keener believes that the

> end-time schemes often included a great battle between the people of the light and the people of darkness, and Jesus certainly expected violence (24:1-2), but His own followers were to stay clear of it.[31]

Note that Jesus only commanded Peter to put his sword back in its place but He did not tell him to throw it away, destroy it, or not to use it again in any situation. In this circumstance, it was wrong to fight, but Jesus was not prohibiting the use of the sword in self-defense, (cf Luke 22:38). Jesus' words seem to apply to mission. While Jesus was with the disciples during His earthly ministry, they were protected from deprivation of life's necessities (9:10-17) and from violent persecution. Just writes, "The period of physical safety is drawing to a close. When Jesus is arrested, the lives of the disciples will be in jeopardy too."[32]

In subsequent church history, the disciples must plan carefully and take precautions if they are to complete their work as God intends (6:46-49; 14:28-30). They will face spiritual enemies and physical need, assault, and martyrdom. They must equip themselves in all respects for the battle ahead. When Paul urges Christians to arm themselves with the full armor of God (Ephesians 6:10-20), he recognizes that true enemies are spiritual, and so the essential weaponry is as well.

Just writes,

---

[30]Keener, *The IVP Bible Background Commentary: New Testament*, 122.

[31]Ibid.

[32]Just, *Concordia Commentary: A Theological Exposition of Sacred Scripture* (Luke 9:51-24:53), 851.

> Yet even though the kingdom of God does not come by the
> sword, physical provisions for the labor of ministry and the
> bodily necessities of those who serve will be required.[33]

Jesus is speaking with great irony. The disciples have exhibited a pattern of misunderstanding throughout their sojourn with him. They still do not comprehend that in the kingdom the things of God are opposite from the things of people.[34] In this respect, they are sinners who think about their own needs and do not trust the Lord of the harvest to provide. They have been sent as messengers of peace, but like Jerusalem (Luke 19:42), they do not yet truly understand the things that make for peace, as shown by the two swords they have in their possession at Passover. They are among the transgressors whom Jesus came to save.[35] Just writes,

> The two swords suggest the apostles were afraid and so
> brought swords to defend themselves by violence. Hence,
> the apostles are among the transgressors. But this citation
> primarily sets the stage for the passion that is to follow. From
> this moment on, Jesus will be reckoned with transgressors.[36]

These precise words conform to Luke's view of Jesus as the suffering, righteous prophet who comes to identify with sinful humanity, place Himself in solidarity with sinners, and die on behalf of all, crucified between two malefactors.[37] The author believes that the passage indicates the hospitality the disciples received then, would not necessarily await them in future. But now, is emphatically a signal of their new situation after the resurrection (Luke 22:36). Let the one

---

[33]Ibid., 852.
[34]Ibid.
[35]Ibid.
[36]Ibid.
[37]Ibid.

who has no sword sell his garment and buy one. This is an indication that to give up a necessary garment for a sword indicates hostility and persecution are at hand (Acts 8:1-3; 9:1-2, 12: 1-5). Jesus warns His disciples about the hostile times they will face, similar to His rejection. No disciple including us will avoid some of the hostility that Jesus faced. Yet, He bore the sins of man, and makes intercession for the transgression (Isaiah 53:12).

His Kingdom is Not of This World
John 18:36

At His trial, Jesus answered:

> My kingdom is not of this world. If my kingdom were of this world, my servants would have been fighting, that I might not be delivered over to the Jews. But my kingdom is not from this world.
>
> —John 18:36

Jesus' clear statement shows that God's kingdom is not defended by force of counter-violence. Rather, He is pointing out specifically that His was a spiritual kingdom. This spiritual kingdom has enough resources of its own to be victorious if it were to be engaged in actual physical violence with the kingdom of the world (Matthew 26:53). Jesus was rejecting any worldly political aspirations or rebellious intent. His kingdom did not threaten the external rule of the Roman Empire (Luke 20:25). If Jesus had been establishing a political kingdom, He would have encouraged His disciples to fight to establish it (18:10-11). Engelbrecht believes that "legitimate public ordinances are good creations of God and divine ordinances, which a Christian can safely use."[38]

---

[38]Engelbrecht, *The Study Bible, English Standard Version*, 1820.

Do Not Murder
Matthew 5:21-23

One of the most revolutionary teachings of Jesus is that human violence starts in a deeper place. The mind of violence has already begun before blood is spilled or words wound. In the Sermon on the Mount, Jesus said,

> You have heard that it was said to those of old, "you shall not murder, and whoever murders will be liable to judgment." But I tell you anyone who is angry with his brother must answer in court.

We cannot talk about murder without talking about rage. We cannot talk about burning of churches, bombings, and taking of lives in Northern Nigeria without talking about the infections of hatred, malice, and anger in a violent culture. Again, there is this important teaching from Mark 7:14:

> Then He called the people again and said to them, "Listen to this: nothing that comes from the outside into a person can make him unclean, but what comes out of a person makes him unclean."

Here is the crux of the matter and it is the ugly news of the human condition that violence, like all sins, comes out of the human heart. Violence appears not to be caused by what people see or in movies. External stimuli certainly affect people. Deep psychological wounding also conditions people. A culture of violence tends to give permission to be violent, and or to be desensitized, but the instinct and choice to act out in violence comes out of the heart. We are not saying that this statement of Jesus offers a complete psychology for violence. Nevertheless, there is a kernel of truth here as we look at the mystery of violence in our society, especially in context of Christians in Northern

Nigeria. This focus on the internal sinful motivation for violence is in complete contrast to the approach adopted by both Pharisees and Muslims.-who believe that violence and sin is something external hence all of the rules and regulations to try and prevent it.

Faithful in the Face of Violence
Matthew 10:28

This aspect leads to Jesus encouraging us to live bravely in the face of violence. Jesus clearly taught that the world is a sinful and violent place, yet He challenged His followers not to live in fear and trepidation. They are encouraged not to be afraid of those who kill the body but cannot kill the soul. He also encourages His followers that in the world, they will have trouble, but they are to be brave because He has conquered the world (John 16:33). In the context of the religious violence in Northern Nigeria, what is this bravery of which Jesus speaks? How does this kind of bravery affect Evangelical members and others living everyday lives and working in a violent place like Northern Nigeria and other parts of the world where religious violence prevails? How can they take Jesus' teaching to heart so that they do not live their lives cowering? We shall turn to the next chapter to examine religion and peace building.

CHAPTER 6

RELIGION AND PEACE BUILDING

Then Joshua made a treaty of peace with them to let them live,
and the leaders of the assembly ratified it by oath.

—Joshua 9:15-16

In context of Nigeria, religious actors and leaders have been involved in local peace building efforts, policy makers, diplomats and scholars approach religion not only as a source of conflict, but as an important resource in resolving conflict and violence. However, more work is needed on religions beyond Christianity and Islam in Nigeria. John Paul Lederach, in a lifetime's collection reflecting on peace building using *The Moral Imagination*, asked a simple, but clear question "How do we transcend the cycles of violence that bewitch our human community while still living in them?" His response to this question is that we "generate, mobilize, and build moral imagination . . . which requires the capacity to imagine ourselves in a web of relationships that includes our enemies . . ."[1] Gordon S. Smith and Harold Coward, describe,

---

[1]Lederach, John Paul. *The Moral Imagination: The Art and Soul of Building Peace* (Oxford and New York: Oxford University Press, 2005),5.

> Religious peace building as the range of activities performed
> by religious actors and institutions for the purpose of resolving
> and transforming deadly conflict, with social relations and
> political institutions characterized by an ethos of tolerance and
> nonviolence.[2]

Peace building is a requirement for freedom from both internal and external conflict. Having security from external enemies, as well as calmness of mind for those who put faith in God is inclusive (Isaiah 26:12; Job 22:21; Isaiah 26:3). Peace is so pleasing to God that the righteous are required to pursue it earnestly (Psalm 34:14). Jesus is the foundation of peace. "Blessed are the peacemakers, for they will be called children of God," (Matthew 5:9). What can Christians do about violence? It appears that they must start with a serious commitment to the principle of "blessed are the peacemakers." However, it seems that will not happen unless we go beyond wishful thinking.

Nevertheless, the question remains: what is this peacemaking? Peace building is active work, hard work, and frustrating work. It is not the convenient thing. Does it not mean blessed are those who expend their lives in the interest of reconciliation and shalom? France comments,

> This beatitude goes beyond a merely peaceful disposition
> to an active attempt to 'make' peace, perhaps by seeking
> reconciliation with one's enemies, but also more generally
> by bringing [peace and reconciliation?] To those who are
> estranged from one another.[3]

---

[2]Smith, Gordon S. and Harold Coward, eds, *Religion and Peace Building* (Albany, New York: State University of New York Press, 2004), 5.

[3]France, R. T. *The Gospel of Matthew* (Grand Rapids: William B. Eerdmans Publishing Company, 2007), 169.

Peace building is a means of involvement in [the] human predicament of war-like conditions. Coping with such conditions corresponds to God's own response and action. It implies assuming responsibility against all the odds, risking peacemaking out of the situation of powerlessness, and demonstrating the conviction that in the end God's kingdom will prevail. The challenge is not palatable. However, it is Jesus' clear call for His followers at all times. Somehow, the message and work of peace builders need to have begun long before the bullets are loaded for violence. David Gooding and John Lennox wrote,

> In the first century, Christians obeyed Christ's prohibition on the use of the sword either to promote Christianity or to defend it. Nowhere in the whole of Acts has Luke recorded that the Christians started any of the riots themselves or even retaliated against those who frequently attacked or persecuted them.[4]

> As far as Christendom is concerned, it has not been faithful adherence to the basic doctrines of the Bible that has caused the all-too-frequent intolerance, political discrimination and bloodshed in the name of religion.[5]

How about evoking counter-violence? In the Old Testament, the author suggested that personal rights are protected by a divinely established system of retribution. Since the community of believers is not a national nation as Israel, there is no room in Jesus' model for retaliation.

Learning from Gooding's explanation, the way to overcome evil is obedience; to let it not lead to retaliating because it does not result in peace. However, violence stands unacceptable for its failure to propel counter-violence. Gooding wrote,

---

[4]Gooding, David and John Lennox. *The Definition of Christianity* (Bukuru, Nigeria: Africa Christian Textbooks/Myrtlefield House, 2014), 89.
[5]Ibid.

> It has been sheer disobedience to Christ's prohibition of the use
> of the sword, or of violence of any kind or to protect the cause
> of Christ, or to increase the church…[6]

Jesus forbade His disciples to indulge in personal retaliation of any sort. Stumme rightly observes that our Christian witness "takes on a critical edge when we trust our moral activity to achieve what comes only as God's gift of faith."[7] This biblical and theological imperative may remind us Christians in Northern Nigeria that our relationship with God is not something we can earn through our own energy, but it is God's gift to which we respond in faith.

The heart of Christians' response to violence is to clarify, reinforce, restore, and promote an understanding of God's gracious gift through bearing witness to Jesus Christ and remaining firm in the theology of carrying the cross of suffering and constantly following Him. Briscoe warns Christians that "the reality of conflict in human relations is that evil will continue to persist and Christians will not be exempt from its painful encroachment."[8] The New Testament idea shows that with the teaching and example of Jesus Christ, God's clear will for Christians in a violent world is for them to stand firm in their faith. Atkinson points out that the New Testament response of peacemaking, patient suffering, non-retaliation - even for an unjust cause, and overcoming evil with good, dominates the text.[9] Wink reiterates,

> For Christians, nonviolence is rooted in our understanding of a
> God who is peace, who gives peace, who calls us to make peace

---

[6] Ibid.

[7] Stumme, John R. "A Tradition of Christian Ethics," in *The Promise of Lutheran Ethics*, eds., Karen L. Bloomquist and John R. Stumme (Minneapolis: Augsburg Fortress, 1998), 1.

[8] Briscoe, D. Stuart. *The Communicator's Commentary: Romans* (Waco: Word Book Publishers, 1982), 228.

[9] Atkinson, *New Dictionary of Christian Ethics and Pastoral Theology*, 878.

> and justice, and to live out Jesus's teachings and bear witness to
> the promise of God.[10]

From the Acts of the Apostles, the suffering of the church has greater witnessing power than the Word alone (Acts 3-8).

The secondary motifs in the New Testament remind Christians that some people of God may find themselves in military or police posts (Acts 10). Moreover, God intends to use those who bear the sword to punish evil and protect the good (Romans 13:3-5). This is already realized in God's established kingdom through Jesus Christ (Luke 24:39; John 4:24; Romans 8:20-23; 1 Corinthians 11:25; 2 Corinthians 3:6; Hebrews 9:15, 12:24).

The New Testament reveals that Jesus gives gifts to the church for spiritual power and not for militant response to violence (Ephesians 4:7-13). The Christians' battleground is in the spiritual realm against the forces of Satan and spiritual warfare by putting on the full power of God's own spiritual armor (Ephesians 6:12-13).[11] Jesus never defined the mission of the New Testament church by conquest of land and or people. Instead, its mission is to encourage the free submission of souls to the will of God and to recognize the dignity of all human beings as bearers of God's image in which all carnal weapons are renounced (Matthew 26:50-56; 2 Corinthians 10:4,5). The New Testament teaching clearly shows that a violent end awaits Satan and his cohorts at the end of human history (Revelation 19:11-15; 20:1-10). Schulz concludes, "The church must learn to listen in order to respond to cries and the crises of our time."[12]

---

[10]Wink, Walter. *Living Faithfully in a Violent World: Walking with Jesus' Path of Peace* (Minneapolis: Augsburg Fortress, 2001), 11.

[11]Kunhiyop, Samuel Waje. *African Christian Ethics* (Grand Rapids: Zondervan and World Alive Publishers, 2004), 115.

[12]Schulz, Klaus Detlev. *Mission from the Cross*, 301.

CHAPTER 7

EARLY CHURCH RESPONSE

When Jesus was born, his birth triggered religious and political strife. Herod was afraid and his response was to attempt to have the newly born King of the Jews executed (Matthew 2:3- 18).The early growth of the Christian church was likewise confronted with a systematic attempt to suppress or exterminate Christianity with differing methods ranging from social pressure up to and including systematic violence being used. Violence against Christians began with the action of the Sanhedrin against Peter and John in reprisal for their proclamation of the resurrection of Jesus Christ (Acts 4:1-3, 5). Violence took place when Stephen was stoned to death, following which the Christians of Jerusalem were driven out of the city and scattered in every direction (Acts 8:1-4). Harrison writes that,

> Diocletian attempted not only to exterminate the Christians, but also to destroy their literature. He confiscated and burned all copies of the Scriptures that he found and demolished the church buildings.[1]

---

[1]F. Harrison, Everett. *Dictionary of Theology* (Grand Rapids: Baker Book House, 1960), 403.

Violence thus characterized the beginning of the church. The pagans misunderstood the Christians. They considered Christians to be atheists, anti-social, and politically subversive. Violence was the protest of heathenism against the gospel in its spiritual and social manifestation.[2] So how did Christians respond to the violence used against them down through the centuries? Johnson notes,

> Jesus's response to religious violence of the first century was often ignored, but never forgotten. Even when the church herself persecuted Christian heretics, Jews, and Muslims, some Christians still struggled to bear witness to the peace mandate of their Lord.[3]

Indeed, Johnson further argues that "the Christian religion was spread by violence [by non-Christians] beginning with the apostles and their followers."[4]

Hecht notes,

> Frequently, early Christians who refused to renounce their faith in Christ literally were fed to the lions. They had no armies and conquered no lands by force in the name of Christianity for centuries after Christ established His church.[5]

The Christian church was often subjected to violence.[6] Dadang records a prayer that Clement, an elder in the Church at Rome, wrote during Nero's violent attacks against early Christians. Polycarp, as a faithful cross-bearer, was burnt at the stake for refusing to renounce his

---

[2]Ibid.

[3]Johnson, Roger A. *Peacemaking and Religious Violence: From Thomas Aquinas to Thomas Jefferson* (Cambridge: The Lutterworth Press, 2011), 2.

[4]Hecht, Bill. *Two Wars: We Must Not Lose* (Fort Wayne: Concordia Theological Seminary, 2012), 17.

[5]Ibid.

[6]Ibid.

faith in response to violent acts against him. Cairns maintain that "Polycarp was a valuable witness to the early church even to death."[7] These are examples that the early church was mainly nonviolent and consciously pacifist. No circumstances justified a Christian use of force. "Tertullian demanded a connection between Christian teaching and practical moral life."[8] "His philosophy on pacifism has been a subject of debate."[9] Witness for Christ in the midst of violence was common among early Christians. They chose to die for their faith. Hurlbut rightly captions it that

> The most prominent fact in the history of the church through the second and third centuries is the [violence] persecution of Christianity by the Roman emperors.[10]

As a plan and practice, pacifism was applied in response to religious violence from the first through the third centuries of Christianity based on the teaching of Jesus to respond to any form of violent activity against Christians in nonviolent manner. Dadang further wrote

> while this condition was not continuous, it was often repeated for years at a time, and liable to break forth at any moment in terrible forms. It lasted into the fourth century until 313 A.D., when the Edict of Constantine …ended all attempts to destroy the church of Christ.[11]

Their witnessing life and their theology of the cross began to give way from the fourth century.

---

[7] Ibid.
[8] Ibid.
[9] Ibid.
[10] Ibid.
[11] Ibid.

Contemporary Responses

Huntington argues that religion is a cause of violence and that "religion is a central culprit, pointing to the irrational, absolute and divisive character of religious faith, particularly that of extremists or fundamentalists."[12] Pape and Cavanaugh, note that religion plays a major role in international violence and terrorism and that religious fundamentalism or intense faith makes violence more likely or lethal.[13]

Barkun, however, opposes connecting religious violence with fundamentalism. He argues that

> Attempts to screen religious groups for violence by checking for fundamentalism ignores the fact that both the history of fundamentalism and the practice of the vast majority of contemporary groups identified as fundamentalists are decidedly nonviolent and that the reality is that religious beliefs alone are a poor indicator of any propensity to violence.[14]

Arnett points out that "conflict is an inevitable moral part of living that cannot and should not be eliminated."[15] However, Arnett maintains that,

---

[12]Huntington, *The Clash of Civilizations and the Changing World Order* (New York: Simon and Schuster, 1996), 96, 209-211, 254.

[13]Pape, Robert A. *Dying to Win: The Strategic Logic of Suicide Terrorism* (New York: Random House, 2005), 46.

[14]Barkun, Michael. "Religious Violence and the Myth of Fundamentalism," *Totalitarian Movement and Political Religions 4*, no. 3 (2003): 55-70. David Harrington Watt equally offers similar objections to the misguided understanding of fundamentalism in "The Meaning and End of Fundamentalism," Religious Studies Review 30, no. 4 (2004), 271-274.

[15]Arnett, Ronald C. *Dwell in Peace: Applying Nonviolence to Every Relationship* (Elgin: The Brethren Press, 1980), 13.

the common way to deal with conflict in interpersonal relationships is with some form of violence or the violation of another's dignity without being oppressed.[16]

Culver, arguing from a nuclear point of view, writes

pacifist doctrine does not lead to peace but anarchy and chaos, because today's leading pacifists' ideas are often based purely on tradition, and ignoring that in a fallen world, often the only way to peace is through defensive strength.[17]

Pilar and Dietmar say,

Much space exists between realism or national security that dismisses all talk of moral restraints in violence as sentimental, and those who in the name of nonviolence or peace deny the possibility of any moral legitimacy to violence.[18]

In advocating a just response to violence, Eckhart and Aron argue,

The legitimacy and illegitimacy of using force are to be defined in such a way that they remain open for variations of the divine action.[19]

Griffith points out, "Augustine and Ambrose's justification of violence is the reason for current involvement of Christian groups in sectarian violence."[20] The discussion of violence by scholars reveals that there

---

[16]Ibid.

[17]Culver, Robert Duncan. *The Peace Mongers: A Biblical Answer to Pacifism and Nuclear Disarmament* (Wheaton: Tyndale House Publishers, 1985), 29.

[18]Aquino, Maria Pilar and Mieth Dietmar. *The Return of Just War* (London: SCM Press, 2001/2), 89.

[19]Eckhart, Lorenz. *Justice through Violence: Ethical Criteria for Legitimate Use of Force* (Geneva: The Lutheran World Federation, 1984), 9. See also Raymond Aron, *The Century of Total War* (Boston: Fortress Press, 1955), 57.

[20]Griffith, Lee. *The War on Terrorism and the Terror of God* (Grand Rapids: Eerdmans, 2003), 20-23, 134-135.

are those who favor a violent response to violence. Others favor the tradition and theology of nonviolence as a Christian resource in the struggle against and in response to violence.

Nonviolent Response

Carter believes that

> ...violence in the Old Testament does not mean God teaches us these days to resolve around armaments that depend on weapons capable of wiping out human race.[21]

Long says, "Rather it should be to promote a general well-being of people to overcome hostility and adopt compassion and reconciliation."[22] Haak maintains, "We alone are responsible for controlling this violence. When it is confronted with violence, a society may decide against its use."[23]

Daschke and Kille say, "Religion and violence have a complicated relationship to sustain the argument that 'the Bible made me do it.'"[24] Hengel states that the position of Jesus and the early Christians on the question of violence was radically different from that of the zealots, because Jesus' model of nonviolence demanded that His followers renounce violence and love their enemies.[25] Vanderhaar supports this view and notes, "The gospels do not portray Jesus as a zealot, eager for

---

[21]Swaim, J. Carter. *War: Peace and the Bible* (Maryknoll: Orbis Books, 1982), 115,116.

[22]Long, Edward Leroy. *Peace Thinking in a Warring World* (Philadelphia: The Westminster Press, 1983), 98.

[23]Haak, Robert D. "Mapping Violence in the Prophets: Zechariah 2," in the *Aesthetics of Violence in the Prophets*, eds. Julia M. O'Brien and Chris Franke (New York: T&T Clark, 2010), 29-30.

[24]Daschke, Dereck and Andrew Kille. "A Cry Instead of Justice: The Bible and Cultures of Violence" in *Psychological Perspective* (London: T&T Clark, 2010), 14.

[25]Hengel, Martin. *Victory over Violence: Jesus and Revolutionists* (Philadelphia: Fortress Press, 1973), 88.

the violent overthrow of Roman occupation."[26] Tsetsis points out that for a Christian, the issue at stake is not so much the combat against violence, but the elimination of the things that provoke violence.[27] Irvin insists that one of the principles for reconciliation and peace is a commitment to refuse to sanction violence as a holy act.[28] Hauerwas argues that, "Christians are told by our Lord Savior that we must prepare for death because we refuse to kill in the name of survival."[29] Merton[30] and Dear[31] argue that nonviolence is the Christian response to contemporary violence.

De Gruchy[32] and Biggar[33] suggest that forgiveness and reconciliation could help resist, overcome, and recover from violence. Chapman argues that a Christian pastoral theology provides the resources to address the underlying cause of religious violence.[34]

---

[26]Vanderhaar, Gerard A. *Christians and Nonviolence in the Nuclear Age* (Mystic: Twenty-Third Publications, 1982), 53.

[27]Tsetsis, Georges. "Non-Violence in Orthodox Tradition," in *Violence and Christian Spirituality: An Ecumenical Conversation*, ed. Emmanuel Clapsis (Geneva: WCC Publications, 2007), 61.

[28]Irvin, Dale. "The Terror of History and the Memory of Redemption: Engaging the Ambiguities of the Christian Past," in *Surviving Terror: Hope and Justice in a World of Violence*, eds. Victoria Lee Erickson and Michelle Lim Jones (Grand Rapids: Brazos Press, 2002), 53.

[29]Hauerwas, Stanley. "Christian Non-Violence," in *Strike Terror No More: Theology, Ethics and the New War*, ed. Jon L. Berquist (Saint Louis: Chalice Press, 2002), 246-247.

[30]Merton, Thomas. *Peace in the Post-Christian Era* (Maryknoll: Orbis Books, 2004).

[31]Dear, John. *Living Peace: A Spirituality of Contemplation and Action* (New York: Doubleday, 2001).

[32]De Gruchy, John W. *Reconciliation: Restoring Justice* (Minneapolis: Fortress Press, 2002).

[33]Susin, Luiz Carlos and Maria Pilar Aquino, eds., *Reconciliation in a World of Conflicts* (London: SCM, 2003), 7-134.

[34]Chapman Jr., G. Clarke. "Terrorism: A Problem for Ethics or Pastoral Theology?" *Cross Currents* 54 (2004) 120-137.

Kreider et al. believe that for Christians, resurrection today can mean that God's power of peace and life has overcome and is overcoming the power of violence and death.[35] Chernus maintains that, "even if they should lose their lives, they know that they do so in a winning cause."[36] Thus, Christianity prepared adherents to accept war and other adversity as a necessary part of the intensification of evil that must take place during the end times, just as Jesus had provided the model by accepting His death on the cross.[37]

Observation

The early Christian church was pacifist at the beginning. When Christianity was the official religion of the Roman Empire, Christians saw it as their duty not only to protect her existence, but also to protect others. Hence, contemporary views of response to persecution and suffering today do not differ significantly from the early church.

---

[35]Kreider, Alan, Eleanor Kreider, and Paulus Widjaja. *A Culture of Peace: God's Vision for the Church* (Intercourse, Pennsylvania: Good Books, 2005), 140.

[36]Chernus, Ira. *American Nonviolence: The History of an Idea* (Maryknoll: Orbis Books, 2004), 96.

[37]Ibid.

CHAPTER 8

BIBLICAL RESPONSE TO RELIGIOUS VIOLENCE

The problem of violence begins from the Old Testament and provides a starting point for understanding the response to religious violence:

First, the Hebrew Scriptures are not a primer on violence. Rather, with surprising fullness and diversity, they provide guidance for overcoming violence and guide readers to hinder, reject, prevent, and eliminate its causes. The Old Testament portrays violence as abnormal and pathological. Neither the original creation of Genesis 1-2 nor the eventual new creation Revelation 21-22 has any place for violence. Second, the Old Testament literature gives hope of an ultimate end to violence, so Yahweh is said to have worked violence that belongs to the enforcement of His sovereignty (Genesis 3:15; Galatians 4:4). Third, therefore, violence is not part of creation. Rather, violence is a result of the chaos, alienation, and the pride of fallen humanity (Genesis 3:1-14). Fourth, the prophets continued with the announcement of the future coming of the Prince of Peace, who will establish the new kingdom of peace (Isaiah 4:2, 9.6; Micah 4:3; Joel 3:9-10).

In the New Testament literature, violence is replaced by creative, nonviolent alternatives (Romans 8:20-23). It is observed with the patient suffering and forgiving love already realized and experienced in

God's established kingdom through Jesus Christ (Hebrews 9:15; John 3:16; Luke 24:39; John 4:24). God's established kingdom through Jesus Christ never defined the mission of the church by conquest of land and people. Violence results from and manifests in human sin and rebellion against the Creator (Genesis 3; Romans 3:23, 6:23). This position comes from the teaching of Jesus Christ in Matthew 5 and other passages from the Gospels (Luke 6:20-23, 27-31). Rather, Scripture fulfilled Christ's death as foretold in the Old Testament. Jesus Christ has fully exhibited God's will in a violent world (John 1:29-34, 19:30), calling Christians to peacemaking and patient suffering. In Jesus Christ the ethnic and spiritual barriers, the hostility that has separated Jews and Gentiles is broken down (Ephesians 2:14).

A violent ending awaits Satan and his cohorts at the end of human history (Revelation 19:11-15; 20:1-10). From the beginning of early Christianity, the author established the early church's response to religious violence through the first three centuries. The early church was mainly harmless, nonviolent, and consciously pacifist.

When Christianity became the official religion of the Roman Empire, the church saw it as its duty not to only protect her own existence, but to protect others. This spurred Augustine to come up with the "just war" theory and to advocate self-defense as well as fighting for those who could not defend themselves. We further examined current scholarship that contributes in providing the insight that helps guide our responses to the problem of religious violence in our society. Current views of responses to violence and suffering reveal that the Christian pilgrimage is not about the race of saints along the way to heaven, nor of the dangers and encouragement of the pilgrim, but rather a discussion of the qualifications needed to enter the gate at the end of the journey (1 Timothy 2:1-5).

Theological Principles for Response to Religious Violence

The question is what is a proper Biblical theology of suffering, persecution, and response to religious violence? Violence, sufferings, persecution, and death did not originate in the twenty-first century as documented throughout this book. Not only are violence, suffering, persecution, and death not new, they have not yet ceased. As Christians, we look to the final consummation of the kingdom as the ultimate remedy and end to the world's problems. Political and humanitarian efforts may heal certain symptoms of violence, but they cannot cure the underlying disease of sin and its cause. Eitel rightly notes,

> It is thus easy for an Evangelical compassion for people and their eternal destinies to embrace . . . Moody's image of seeking to pull into the heavenly lifeboat as many souls as possible [including the likely vessel of Muslims violence] away from the sinking ship of this world.[1]

We are not saying the principles we are about to mention on the Biblical theology of suffering, persecution, and response to religious violence are final. However, this work suggests that there are four distinctive suggestive Christian missiological concerns about suffering and violence in regards to Islamic-inspired violence in particular.

The first missiological principle is that all Christians belong to the heavenly kingdom irrespective of class, ethnic or economic distinctions (Philippians 3:20). As those who have Christ dwelling in us, we suffer and rejoice together and His identity compels us to live in peace and comfort in violent situations (Romans 12:15).

---

[1] Eitel, Keith E., ed. *Missions in Contexts of Violence* (Pasadena: William Carey Library, 2008), 20.

The second theological principle is the divine calling Christians have to be salt and light to the world (Matthew 5:16). As Christians, Jesus Christ has defined our agenda, and because we love Him, we are constrained to also embrace the mandate He has given the church. Evangelism and witness to Jesus Christ is one distinctively Christian way of dealing with violence and suffering connected with the Muslim-Christian violence in Northern Nigeria or elsewhere.

The third theological principle is that the Triune God reigns over the entire world. Everything that exists and happens in this world is under God's sovereignty. Christians can thus approach violence, sufferings, persecution, and death with confidence that our heavenly ruler is aware, concerned, and involved (John 19:16).

The fourth theological principle is a holistic approach to ministry that is embodied in social, emotional, physical and spiritual concerns. The most effective response to religious violence is to teach theological truths in the process of discipleship and maturing relationships (Matthew 28:19, 20). Spiritual concepts are developed within the framework of the questions and the concerns of daily life. Discipleship in this context focuses on helping people know God in the midst of difficult circumstances. A theology of the cross and suffering is addressed through Biblical concepts of discipleship. The problem African Christians face is a faith that does not transform so it is hard for them to confront and respond to religious violence positively for absence of being true Disciples of Christ. Hull concludes that,

> We have taught non-discipleship Christianity, and in Scripture
> this Christianity does not exist. Jesus and Paul both taught that
> following Jesus is proof of being a Christian (Luke 9:23-25;
> Philippians 2:1-8).[2]

---

[2]Hull, Bill. *Choose the Life: Exploring a Faith That Embraces Discipleship* (Grand Rapids, Michigan: Barker Books, 2004), 23.

Those who are involved in theological education; clergy who are care givers; and those in para-church settings can take the lead by taking steps to promote an atmosphere of training Christians on how to build relationships with people of other religions without compromising Biblical standards. It will lead theologians and pastoral care givers in training to break barriers that are hindrances and build relationships that lead to peaceful coexistence in a given violent environment.

Another procedure that the church needs to pursue vigorously is in the area of advocacy. The church is called to the ministry of advocacy. Advocacy is a deliberate process, based on demonstrated evidence, to directly influence decision makers, stakeholders and relevant audiences to support and implement actions that contribute to the fulfillment of individuals or group rights thus enabling them to re-gain their freedom. The church has ample opportunity to mobilize its members to speak against human rights abuse, and if church leaders fail to point this out to members, human right abuse will continue. Christian leaders are to be sensitized to understand that effective advocacy is not spontaneous but deliberate. Two modern examples are worth mentioning: Peace Direct Local Voices[3] has advocated for peace through its annual consultation with both Christians and Muslims. It does this by development of advocacy partnerships with religious and traditional leaders. It advocates for a reduction in religiously motivated hate speech. It promotes inter-communal, inter-ethnic and inter-religious harmony using positive religious role models and local media. Secondly, ten years ago, Serving In Mission (SIM), Nigeria introduced interfaith and interdenominational Sports Friends sporting activities to Nigeria. These are effective in engaging large numbers of sporting friends relationships between Christians and Muslims youth.

____

[3]Peace Direct, Local Voices was established for peace in Northern Nigeria and it held consultation with religious leaders and youth in Kano, 2016/2017.

Esther and Mordecai are biblical examples who engaged in deliberate process (Esther 4:1-17). These leaders did not carry arms but they were active and intentional in advocacy. The demonstrated fact was that the Jews were to be exterminated and to that effect, an edict was issued. A copy was sent to Esther (Esther 4:7-8). The implication for our contemporary Christian life in this case study was that Mordecai and Esther were upright and well placed in positions of influence. They were determined to employ the advantages of their positions for the good of their people. The actions that added flavor to their advocacy included fasting and praying. Esther and Mordecai involved others. They equally explored ways to meet with the decision makers, stakeholders and relevant community audiences (Esther 4:15-17; 5:1-8).

Recommendations

The recommendations from this book have two major components. The first is to help theologians, Christians, pastors, missionaries, and leaders who are in the Lord's vineyard in Northern Nigeria; in Africa to understand the reason for their existence in the world, their humanity, and their behaviors as they endure sufferings and cope with the realities and fragility of life. The second is that it will inculcate Biblical awareness not only in members of churches, but also in their theologians and pastors throughout Northern Nigeria, Africa and elsewhere enabling Christians to serve God and live as witnesses to the world. This will help in communicating and preaching the Gospel message in such a way that speaks to contemporary social and spiritual needs answering the questions of life people are asking. God requires total love and commitment from His children of light toward their neighbors who are still in the dark. When they reach the understanding that violent living is counterproductive and self-defeating to existence, it will help them approach better and respond appropriately to religious violence within the context of Jesus' love. It will further help them to understand that resorting to a violent life does not solve any conflict, but rather it suppresses human existence, and prevents peace and church growth. If Christians who are living in flash points of violence are serious in putting into practice the teaching of Jesus to love their neighbors and if they are committed to God, they will shine for Christ without distraction (Philippians 2:16). Then they will experience forgiveness and reconciliation leading to healing and praying constantly for their enemies to have respect for human life and dignity.

Christians in Nigeria, Africa and elsewhere in the world, are reminded of the concluding remarks that McDermott offers. He writes,

> While other religions have truth, they do not know the far fuller truth revealed in and by Christ. [If non-Christians], for example, know about regular prayer and the signs of God in creation, they nevertheless lack assurance of salvation and the fullness of life in the Spirit.[4]

Nor do they know the fullness of the love of God that has been revealed through Christ's crucifixion and resurrection or the glory of the Triune God.[5] God wants to bring them to the fullness of eternal life. Only in Christ is there fully human and fully meaningful life now. Lydia was already worshiping God. However, she came to a fuller experience of divine grace through an encounter with Jesus Christ (Acts 16:14). McDermott further cites Packer,

---

[4]McDermott, Gerald R. *Can Evangelicals Learn From World Religions?* Jesus, Revelation & Religious Traditions (Downers Grove, Illinois: InterVarsity Press, 2000), 213.

[5]Ibid.

> We Christians are commanded by Scripture to share the gospel
> with those who do not know it. It does not matter what we
> think of their future prospects, nor does it matter how much
> truth we think they may have.[6]

We dare not neglect our duty to proclaim if we are to continue to be [Christians] who try to live our lives under Christ and His word.[7] We share the gospel in evangelism and missions out of love and compassion. Non-Christians may know much about God without coming into a saving relationship with Him. The implication of that relationship leads to eternal separation from the only source of love and happiness. For Christians to ignore this problem is an act of cruelty and indifference in a world that needs the love of God. When real war is raging, it is deceptive and heartless to cry Peace, Peace, when there is no peace (Jeremiah 8:11). So out of love for our non-Christians friends, we want to share God's love with them even in the middle of religious violence.

Christians are further reminded according to McDermott,

> This world is a battlefield between the forces of light and the
> forces of darkness. We must therefore, participate in spiritual
> warfare in order to roll back the forces of evil, and our best
> weapon is the gospel.[8]

The author is exhorting Christians in Northern Nigeria; in Africa and elsewhere, to recognize Jesus as Lord and trust Him and always be prepared to give an answer for the reason of their hope with gentleness as part of their suffering for Christ in their context of living in a violent environment (1 Peter 3:15).

---

[6]Ibid., 214.
[7]Ibid.
[8]Ibid., 215.

The Christian pilgrimage is not about the race of saints along the way to heaven, or of the dangers and encouragement of the pilgrim, but rather a discussion of the qualifications needed to enter the gate at the end of the journey.

BIBLIOGRAPHY

Allen, Roland. *Paul's Missionary Methods: In His Time and Ours.* Downers Grove, Illinois: InterVarsity Press Academics, 2012.

Avalos, Hector. *Fighting Wars: The Origins of Religious Violence.* Amherst, New York: Prometheus Books, 2005.

Barth, Hans-Martin. *The Theology of Martin Luther.* Minneapolis: Fortress Press, 2013.

Barrett, David. *World Christian Encyclopedia.* New York: Oxford University Press, 2001.

Best, G. Shedrack. *Conflicts and Peace Building in Plateau State.* Ibadan: Spectrum Books Limited, 2007.

Bicheno, Hugh. *What Does Religion Have to Do with War: An Oxford Companion to the Military History.* Oxford: Oxford University Press, 2004.

Boer, Jan H. *Nigeria's Decades of Blood: Studies in Christian-Muslim Relations.* Jos: Stream Christian Publishers, 2003.

Booth, Wayne C. *The Craft of Research.* Chicago: University of Chicago, 2003.

Cavanaugh, William. *The Myth of Religious Violence: Secular Ideology and the Roots of Modern Conflict.* New York: Oxford University, 2009.

Chernus, Ira. *American Nonviolence: The History of an Idea.* Maryknoll, New York: Orbis Books, 2004.

Chilton, Bruce. *Abraham's Curse: The Root of Violence in Judaism, Christianity and Islam.* New York: Doubleday, 2008.

Cole, Durrell. *When God Says War is Right: The Christian Perspective.* Colorado Springs: Water Back Press, 2002.

Conquest, Robert. *Reflections on a Ravaged Century.* New York, London: W.W. Norton and Company, 2001.

Copan, Paul. *Is God a Moral Monster? Making Sense of the Old Testament God.* Grand Rapids, Michigan: Baker Book House, 2011.

Crampton, Edward Patrick Thurman. *Christianity in Northern Nigeria* With Update by Musa A.B. Gaiya. Bukuru: ACTS. 2004, 2013.

Daschke, Dereck. *A Cry Instead of Justice: The Bible and Cultures in Psychological Perspective.* New York, London: T and T Clark, 2010.

Dietmar, Mieth and Maria Pilar Aquino . *The Return to Just War.* London: SCM Press, 2001/2.

Elford, John R. *The Cambridge Companion to Christian Ethics.* Edited by Robin Gill. Cambridge: Cambridge University Press, 2001.

Engelbrecht, Edward A. *The Study Bible English Standard Version.* Saint Louis: Concordia Publishing House, 2009.

Erickson, Victoria Lee. *Surviving Terror: Hope and Justice in a World of Violence.* Grand Rapids, Michigan: Brazos Press, 2002.

France, R.T. *The Gospel of Matthew.* Grand Rapids, Michigan; Cambridge, UK: William Eerdmans Publishing Company, 2007.

Gehman, Richard. *African Traditional Religion in the Light of the Bible.* Bukuru: ACTS, 2001.

Gibbs, Jeffrey A. *Concordia Commentary: A Theological Exposition of Sacred Scripture Matthew 1:1-11:1.* Saint Louis: Concordia Publishing House, 2006.

Gooding, David and John Lennox. *Definition of Christianity.* Bukuru: ACTS/ Myrtlefield House, 2014.

Gooding, David. *True to the Faith: The Acts of the Apostles: Defining and Defending the Gospel.* Bukuru: ACTS/Myrtlefield House, 2013.

Gofwen, Rotgak I. *Religious Conflicts in Northern Nigeria and Nation Building: The Theories of Two Decades 1980-2000.* Kaduna: Publications of Human Rights Monitors, 2004.

Griffith, Lee. *The War on Terrorism and the Terror of God*. Grand Rapids, Michigan: Eerdmans Publishing House, 2003.

Gutip, Nanwul. *Church Of Christ in Nations. COCIN: Birth and Growth*. Jos: COCIN Printing Press, 2017.

Haak, Robert D. *The Aesthetics of Violence in the Prophets*. New York, London: T and T Clark, 2010.

Hauerwas, Stanley. *In Strike Terror No More: Theology, Ethics and the New War*. Edited by Jon L. Berquist. Saint Louis Missouri: Chalice Press, 2002.

Elliot, Julia, Sara Hawker, and Catherine Soames. *Oxford Dictionary of Current English*. Oxford: Oxford University Press, 2006.

Hecht, Bill. *Two Wars: We Must Not Lose*. Fort Wayne, Indiana: Concordia Theological Seminary, 2012.

Inrig, Gary. *Forgiveness*. Grand Rapids, Michigan: Discovery House Publishers, 2005.

Jacobsen, Douglas. *The World's Christians*. United Kingdom: Willey-Blackwell, 2007.

Johnson, Roger A. *Peacemaking and Religious Violence: From Thomas Aquinas to Thomas Jefferson*. Cambridge, UK: The Lutterworth Press, 2011.

Juergensmeyer, Mark. *Terror in the Mind of God: The Global Rise of Religious Violence*. Berkeley: University of California Press, 2001.

Kippenberg, Hans. *Violence as Worship: Religious Wars in the Age of Globalization*. Stanford: Stanford University, 2011.

Kleinig, John W. *Concordia Commentary: A Theological Exposition of Sacred Scripture Leviticus*. Saint Louis: Concordia Publishing House, 2003.

Koschorke, Klaus. *A History of Christianity in Asia, Africa and Latin America 1450-1990*. Grand Rapids, Michigan; Cambridge, UK: William B. Eerdmans Publishing Company, 2007.

Kreider, Alan. *A Culture of Peace: God's Vision for the Church*. Pennsylvania: Good Books, 2005.

Kunhiyop, Samuel Waje. *African Christian Ethics.* Grand Rapids Michigan: Zondervan and World Alive Publishers, 2004.

Lederach, John Paul. *The Moral Imagination: The Art and Soul of Building Peace.* Oxford and New York: Oxford University Press, 2005.

Lee, Griffith. *The War on Terrorism and the Terror of God.* Grand Rapids, Michigan: Eerdmans, 2002.

Long, Edward Leroy. *Peace Thinking in a Warring World.* Philadelphia: The Westminster Press, 1983.

Loves, Yahweh. *The Beginning of the End of Islam on the Plateau.* Jos: Savior's Associates, 2010.

Mandryk, Jason and Patrick Johnstone. *Operation World.* Carlisle: Paternoster, 2010.

Middleton, Richard. *The New Interpreter's Dictionary of the Bible.* Nashville: Abingdon Press, 2009.

Osaghae, E. *A History of Identities, Violence and Stability in Nigeria.* Ibadan: Center for Research and Inequality, 2003.

Pape, Robert A. *Dying to Win: The Strategic Logic of Suicide Terrorism.* New York: Random House, 2005.

Piper, John. *Filling up the Afflictions of Christ.* Wheaton, Illinois: Crossway Books, 2009.

Schulz, Klaus Detlev. *Mission from the Cross: The Lutheran Theology of Missions.* Saint Louis: Concordia Publishing House, 2009.

Selengut, Charles. *Sacred Fury: Understanding Religious Violence.* 2nd ed. Lanham, Maryland: Rowman & Littlefield, 2008.

Sider, Ronald J. *How Should Christians Respond? Strike Terror No More: Theology, Ethics, and the New War.* Saint Louis: Chalice Press, 2002.

Smith, Gordon S. and Harold Coward, eds. *Religion and Peace building.* Albany, New York: State University of New York Press, 2004.

Stern, Jessica. *Terror in the Name of God: Why Religious Militants Kill*. New York: Ecco, 2003.

Sundita, Abbas. *Look behind the Façade: Some Serious Stuff You're Not Supposed to Know about Islam*. USA: Xulon Press, 2006.

Tsetsis, George. *Violence and Christian Spirituality: An Ecumenical Conversation*. Geneva, Switzerland: WCC Publications, 2007.

Thomson, Milburn J. *Justice and Peace: A Christian Primer*. Maryknoll, New York: Orbis Books, 2003.

Walls, Andrew F. *The Cross-Cultural Process in Christian History*. Maryknoll, New York: Orbis Books, 2002.

Waltke, Bruce K. *Old Testament Theology: An Exegetical Canonical and Thematic Approach*. Grand Rapids, Michigan: Zondervan Publishing House, 2007.

Wink, Walter. *Living Faithfully in a Violent World: Walking with Jesus Path of Peace*. Minneapolis: Augsburg Fortress, 2001.

---------------. *Jesus and Nonviolence: A Third Way*. Minneapolis: Fortress Press, 2003.

www.ingramcontent.com/pod-product-compliance
Lightning Source LLC
Chambersburg PA
CBHW050548160726
48003CB00002B/810